KU-157-867

to Antony,

With warm recollections of
his dear father, of his friendship
and our early meetings.

Devotedly

Edward

June 64.

LOOK BACK - LOOK FORWARD

The author, by Stanley Spencer

LOOK BACK
LOOK FORWARD

BY

EDWARD BEDDINGTON-BEHRENS
C.M.G., M.C. and Bar, Ph.D. (Econ.)

*Il faut trouver l'équilibre entre
l'indiscrétion et le silence*

CHRISTIAN MURCIAUX

WORKING MEN'S COLLEGE
34906
LIBRARY

LONDON
MACMILLAN & CO LTD
NEW YORK · ST MARTIN'S PRESS
1963

Copyright © Sir Edward Beddington-Behrens 1963

First Edition May 1963
Revised December 1963

MACMILLAN AND COMPANY LIMITED
St Martin's Street London WC2
also Bombay Calcutta Madras Melbourne

THE MACMILLAN COMPANY OF CANADA LIMITED
Toronto

ST MARTIN'S PRESS INC
New York

PRINTED IN GREAT BRITAIN

To Renée

Foreword

★

ALL my life I think I have had my eyes on the stars. Inspiring causes have made a deep appeal to me, and I have enjoyed working and fighting for them. Above all, I believe in freedom: the freedom of peoples to determine their own destiny, and the freedom of the individual. That is why I hated public school, with its irksome restrictions and the bullying of the weak by the strong. But I have often found men, whom others consider have had a most successful career, who have created so many shackles in their own lives, that they are denied the ordinary freedoms enjoyed by those of more modest ambitions.

Like many others of my generation, I fought in the First World War with the fervour of a crusader. Later I was on the Secretariat of the League of Nations, and shared the hopes and disillusions of its founders. Circumstances forced me to give up the idea of going into politics and to embark instead on a business career. I found the problems of industry and finance a most fascinating study. After many failures, I was fortunate enough to achieve sufficient financial independence to enable me to take an active part in furthering certain causes which had inspired me in my youth.

Interest in music, literature and painting helped to give me a balanced view of life. Disappointments, obstacles and periods of unhappiness, proved in my case to be spurs to greater efforts and endeavour. Character, like steel, is tempered on the hard anvil of life's experiences. Looking back now, I believe that everything that happens widens the horizon, increases the vision, and makes life itself more interesting and enjoyable.

Perhaps now I should explain it all.

Contents

★

Illustrations

★

Acknowledgments

THE author and publishers wish to acknowledge their indebtedness to the following, who have kindly given permission for the use of copyright material: Mr T. S. Eliot, O.M., for the extract from his tribute to Mrs Violet Schiff which appeared in *The Times*, and Professor Jack Isaacs, for the extract from his talk broadcast on the Third Programme in 1949.

PART ONE

Chapter One

★

YOUTH

I WAS born in Paris in 1897, a few minutes after my twin brother Walter; and my parents, unable to decide on a second name for me, christened me Edward Beddington, Beddington being my mother's maiden name.

My father had been established in Paris for a great many years as representative of leading British firms in France, and was President of the British Chamber of Commerce. I can well remember from early childhood the leisurely cultured and social atmosphere that existed in Paris in those pre-war days: Mother's weekly reception day, the etiquette of leaving cards, and social calls. The grand parties Mother used to tell me about the following morning, such as Count Boni de Castellane's last great ball at the Tir au Pigeon Club in the Bois.

Today there is a large foreign colony in Paris, consisting mostly of Americans, but at that time foreign residents like my parents, who spoke French as if it were their own language, found their friends amongst the French and were fully integrated into French society.

I remember going out with Walter and Mother in the victoria, with the coachman and groom in livery on the box in front and the sleek bay horses. On Sundays the carriage would take us to the Bois de Boulogne. Here we would walk in the 'Allée de la Vertue', where Mother would meet her women friends, and Father would ride on the track alongside in morning coat and long, grey riding-trousers, saluting numerous friends with a wide sweep of his top hat.

Mother had a beautiful voice and was a fine musician, able to write a musical score straight off. In those days, so-called amateur musicians worked as hard to perfect themselves as those who had to earn their living by it, for no one seemed in a hurry and there was time and leisure available. Her mother, Zillah Beddington, was an accomplished pianist whose spacious drawing-room in Hyde Park Square was a meeting place for many famous musicians such as Caruso, Kreisler, Lechitinsky, Puccini and Paolo Tosti.

Evelyn, my mother, and two of her three sisters, Sybil and Violet, were known as the beautiful Beddington sisters in their youth. And all three had lovely singing voices. Violet, later Violet Schiff, the youngest sister, was to become my life-long friend. Their eldest sister Ada, later Ada Leverson, was a great friend of Oscar Wilde, who nicknamed her the Sphinx. Her witty novels are currently being rediscovered. Much has been written about her by Osbert Sitwell and she features in numerous books about the life of Oscar Wilde.

Father was a good violinist. He also composed for the violin, and one of his most treasured possessions was a Guarnerius. Some of my earliest recollections are of my mother accompanying my father or working hard at the piano or doing her singing exercises. Probably this is why the sound of people practising music, even dull scales, never disturbs me. It brings back the peace of my childhood. It symbolises for me a way of life devoted to study, not concerned with material gain or worldly ambitions.

Walter and I were devoted to each other, as sometimes happens in the case of twins, when they are brought up together by a loving and understanding mother. We did not look alike, but were of similar build. He had a sweet nature, generous and vulnerable. His values were those of an artist and not of a man of the world, and he looked to me for assistance when it came to practical matters.

He had a voice of wonderful quality. He would sing a song, and straight away its tempo and musical feeling were

My Mother

Father, Mother, and the twins in the Bois de Boulogne, 1902

The author and his twin brother, aged 11

perfect — with that individual interpretation and warmth which characterises the great singers. Paolo Tosti, the composer, who had taught my mother and Violet, always said that he loved teaching Walter his own songs and was amazed at his virtuosity.

I, too, loved music and Mother started to teach me the piano; but she became ill, and was unable to continue my lessons, so I never learned. In later years it is almost impossible to make up for the grounding one can only get in childhood.

My mother was ill over a long period, and finally died when I was thirteen. But her illness brought us more closely together. She treated me not as a boy, but as a trusted friend to whom she could confide her most intimate thoughts. Mother, missing the companionship of her sisters and obliged, owing to her illness, to spend much of her time in bed, found in me a receptive and sympathetic listener. Looking back, I marvel at her frankness in telling me the story of her first marriage, against the will of her parents, to a cousin, which ended tragically, and all about her first husband, whom she had loved far more than my father.

After Mother's death, Walter and I were packed off to a preparatory school, and then to Charterhouse. Father, alone, did not quite know how to cope with children. During the holidays, except for short periods with him at some French watering-place like Deauville or Étretat, we mostly stayed with our uncle and aunt Sydney and Violet Schiff, or with Lord and Lady Herbert Scott. Herbert Scott was a co-director of Father's in the Rolls-Royce company, and an intimate friend of his. We were always most welcome at his home in the country, and many were the happy holidays we spent in their hospitable house.

I hated Charterhouse where, because we had been brought up in France, we were bullied at first as 'froggies'. Robert Graves, in his book *Goodbye to All That*, well describes the sort of unhappy times Walter and I also experienced in our

B

first year. At school Graves was nicknamed 'Von R', and Walter, he and I shared the fun of boxing together. When Walter and I were still under sixteen we won the junior and senior boxing at our weights. If we were drawn to fight each other, a toss of the coin would decide the winner. After that bullying, of course, ceased.

One man at Charterhouse I have always remembered with gratitude was my form master, the Reverend Lancelot J. Allen. At an impressionable age he helped me to understand the strength and comfort of prayer and to appreciate the value of social work, through the activities of the Charterhouse Mission in Bermondsey.

Recalling Allen's kindness to me, I should mention that I had never realised my Jewish origin until a chance remark by another boy at my French day-school, when I was eleven, made me aware of it. Then I discovered the family history from questioning my father. Mother's family originated in Spain. One of her ancestors, Don Caesar Orobio, was burnt at the stake by the Inquisition at Seville at the beginning of the seventeenth century, having been convicted of secretly observing the traditions and faith of Judaism. His son, Don Balthasar Orobio de Castro, born in 1620, was physician and privy councillor to Louis XIV and a friend of Spinoza. During the reign of Charles II his descendants emigrated to the old British colony of Jamaica, where they had sugar estates near Montego Bay. Because it held radical views, the family was nearly ruined by liberating their slaves a year before the Abolition of Slavery Act of 1833, thus forfeiting the compensation paid to slave-owners by the government. For that reason my great-grandfather John Simon was sent to England to read for the Bar. After a successful career as a Q.C., he became Sergeant-at-Law, was knighted and for twenty-five years was Liberal member for Dewsbury in the House of Commons.

My father's family emigrated from Hamburg at the end of the Napoleonic wars and established textile businesses in

Manchester and Bradford. The Bradford business of Sir Jacob Behrens and Sons is still flourishing, carried on from father to son for the last hundred and forty years. Though Sir Jacob was a deeply religious man, he took no part in Jewish religious observances, nor was he drawn to any conventional religion. None of his descendants ever had any interest in the Jewish religion and some became Quakers. A member of the family, Sir Charles Behrens, was Lord Mayor of Manchester at the turn of the century.

Though proud of my origin, I have never considered my loyalties or sympathies other than completely British; and have always chosen my friends for their human qualities, or for interests shared in common, irrespective of race or nationality.

There are, of course, many inherent differences between the descendants of Jewish families who, because they lived in countries where the Jews were not oppressed, had wealth and position and leisure for education and culture, and those who more recently escaped from the harsh oppression in the ghettos of Eastern Europe. Many of the latter, though now wealthy, continue to live a ghetto-like existence of their own choosing in England and eschew assimilation, an attitude which is very understandable.

It was through my young English master, Mallory, who was later to die near the summit of Mount Everest, that I began to understand and admire the drawings of Michelangelo. The walls of his rooms were covered with reproductions from the Sistine Chapel. I remember his enormous physical strength, his Greek profile, and how he used to climb trees and jump from one to another like a monkey. He was an extremely sensitive and cultured man, and despite his athletic build was unmercifully teased by the boys. Someone had seen him with one of the pretty girls who served in a teashop called Astolats. This led to the boys constantly quoting from a poem by Tennyson about Lancelot and Elaine, the lily maid of Astolat, which always made him blush. This incident is an illustration of the peculiar cruelty of young boys when gathered together.

Walter was no good at lessons and left Charterhouse at sixteen, having spent a record period in the lower school. He then went to a delightful school at Avenches, the old capital of Switzerland.

I had no difficulties of this kind, was moved up every term, and got school colours for boxing and swimming; but I left two terms later to join my brother, with the idea of learning languages.

Our Swiss school was situated near the Lake of Morat, in the lower hills of the Canton de Vaud, a part of Switzerland still untouched by tourists. Avenches is a mediaeval walled town whose church is largely built from old Roman sculptured stone. The headmaster, Monsieur Grau, was tall, middle-aged and very imposing looking. He had in fact in his early youth aspired to be an actor at the Comédie Française and he looked very much the part, whilst declaiming the lofty alexandrines of the tragedies of Corneille and Racine to his pupils.

Father had given him one of his silk-faced frock coats which he used to wear with his top hat when leading the school to church on Sundays. Everybody saluted everybody else in this old-fashioned village, and as 'old Grau' was chairman of the Village Parish Council, he was always addressed as 'Monsieur le Président'. Learning of his harmless foibles, Father used to address his letters to him as 'Monsieur le Dr. Grau' and Grau would leave these envelopes about to give the impression that he had a university degree. In return he addressed his letters to Father 'Monsieur le Chevalier' as Father was a Chevalier de la Légion d'Honneur!

After Charterhouse such a school was a delight. No marks and no exams, and as the school was small, one had a happy relationship with the masters who took a personal interest in one's studies.

It was here I first took up cross-country running. I would look at some distant place on the horizon and decide to run there and back in a straight line. I thought nothing of running twenty miles or so, just to keep fit and get tough — naturally alone, as I could not find anyone to share this unusual taste for long distances. Equipped only with a pair of running shoes, shorts and a sweater, running gave me a wonderful feeling of freedom and exhilaration. I felt I could go anywhere propelled by my own strength, without the mechanical aids of civilisation or wealth. Running up and down hill, hurdling over hedges, in all weathers, made me enjoy something primitive and satisfying. I never felt lonely going for long runs. On the contrary, it stimulated quiet thought and I often had intense imaginary conversations with anyone I was thinking about at the time. And if I was unduly worried, after a run in the countryside my mind would be rested and the arduous exercise would help me to see my problems in proper perspective. I continued this habit of running until I was sixty and had a ski-ing accident. When I lived in a town I always made sure of being near a park, so that I have been able to go for a run most mornings of my life.

I first learned to ski at Avenches, though we did not have steel edges in those days, and the only turn was the telemark. But one learned to jump as soon as one started ski-ing, and this was good practice for going down straight and steep.

Whilst in Switzerland, I was able to devote much more time to working at painting and drawing, and even thought of becoming a painter. During one of my summer holidays in Paris I went to work at the famous Académie Julian. But I soon discovered that I had only an agreeable talent, without any creative originality. The result of this early study has been to give me a lifelong interest in painting and its technical problems, which has helped me to appreciate it all the more.

When war broke out Walter and I were only seventeen.

We returned to England and joined the Cavalry Squadron of the Inns of Court Officers' Training Corps as troopers.

Part of our job was to groom three horses each. This made me very careful in later life not to bring a horse back in a dead sweat, knowing the hard work involved for the groom. I also learned to be quite handy with the lance, a most unwieldy weapon at full speed.

When just eighteen, Walter and I were gazetted as second-lieutenants in a Territorial field-artillery regiment. We went to Thetford in Norfolk for our training, which was pleasant, but rather rudimentary — and at the time I was afraid the war would be over before I got to the front.

Having learned that if I went to the Royal Military Academy at Woolwich (nicknamed the Shop), I would be sent to France within a fortnight of passing out, and that the shortened course only took seven months, I resigned my commission and went to the Shop. There at any rate I could learn to be an efficient officer, which was difficult in my easy-going Territorial regiment. Liking army life, and with no fixed ideas about my future, I decided to become a professional soldier.

I thoroughly enjoyed the comradeship of the Shop and was lucky enough to win a leading riding competition. I felt I had reached the highest pinnacle of my whole military career when, as under-officer, I gave the drill orders on the last parade as the cadets marched past Lord Kitchener.

This parade was preceded by much anxiety. On the night before passing-out there was always the traditional rag, when the officers kept well out of the way to let the Gentlemen Cadets have their fun. I joined other mountaineers in climbing the flagpost on the highest roof of the building and there installing a chamber-pot. This did not look so good the next morning when preparations were being made for the great Kitchener parade — and those concerned were in fear of not being gazetted, especially as a few well-aimed rifle-shots failed to dislodge the offending article which, being made of tin, remained on its perch despite bullet-holes. However, the hose of the local fire-brigade achieved the desired effect just in time: so we were saved.

One of the ordeals one was put through at the Shop was to walk along a narrow plank, high up on top of the gym. Though there was a net far below, it was a particularly frightening experience, which has now been abolished, along with other tests of a somewhat primitive nature. A good result of Shop discipline was that it made me punctual for the rest of my life. There was a ten-minute break when we had to race between distant parade-grounds, which often involved a change of uniform, say from gun-drill jeans into riding kit. Any lateness on parade or even a button left undone was paid for by 5.30 a.m. pack-drills under an irate sergeant. Ever since I have always managed to bath and change into evening dress within ten minutes.

I was keen to start a club to study military campaigns, but the Commandant had me up and explained that 'subalterns don't need to waste their time learning to be little Napoleons'!

So many books have been written about the mud and carnage of the First World War that I do not wish to add much to those harrowing tales. But looking back I recall the sudden surge of idealism of the young men at that period, born in an age when war on a large scale had been unknown for a hundred years, and when much of the spirit of adventure had been stifled in the wealthier classes by the sanctimonious prosperity of the Victorian age, and in the mass of the people by abject poverty.

I joined a Regular battery of the 4th Division just before the Battle of the Somme. On 1 July 1916 the division had some 10,000 casualties in its attack on Beaumont Hamel. In most of the attacks I was Forward Observation Officer (F.O.O.). The job of the F.O.O. is to move up with the leading battalion headquarters and maintain in working order a telegraph-line laid over the ground from the battery. The F.O.O.'s aim was to direct artillery fire and also to inform the rear of the latest infantry positions, and how the battle was going on. You had to have a very tough team of signallers, as there was no wireless in those days; the wire had to be mended day and night, as it was always being broken by shell-fire. You also had to go 'over the top' with the infantry.

I had a particularly poignant experience early in the battle when I was with the 1st Battalion of the Rifle Brigade. It was a dismal night, and a junior officer who was to take out a burial party between the lines had just been wounded, I offered to take his place and led a party of very frightened men into the darkness and horror of no-man's-land. As Very lights shot up we would freeze our movements, because movements are the only targets that can be discerned at night. I had some casualties among my fatigue party, whose job it was to lift the bodies into a hastily-dug grave and take off the identity discs or any papers that could be sent home.

I noticed a young officer killed with his machine-gun team and surrounded by enemy bodies, and I took a large bundle of letters from the inner lining of his tunic. I returned to the battalion dugout very grateful for a good tot of rum, as the episode had been particularly unnerving, and started to look through the letters and souvenirs to be returned to the families of the fallen. In doing this I came across the young officer's packet of letters. These proved to be most romantic. I said to the battalion commander 'It makes dying almost worthwhile, to have lived and inspired such a love'.

He looked through them and tore them up, exclaiming 'You must never send letters like that home as one does not know the circumstances. It might do great harm.'

I was very indignant, thinking him just cynical, and took the girl's address, intending to see her on my next leave to explain the sad circumstances. And for months afterwards I kept thinking of those letters and idealising the love that had inspired them. It was over a year before I was able to get in touch with the girl, on a long-distance telephone call from London. She had just got engaged! Having fallen in love with the idea of what appeared to me a perfect romance as expressed in those letters, I felt as if it was I who had been jilted. My ideal was shattered.

I went through all the battles of the Somme and my regiment supported the Guards Division in the attack on Delville Wood, where I was F.O.O. with the Grenadier Guards battalion on the day on which Harold Macmillan was wounded.

During the war my one wish was to be at the front. I felt that if I came through it would be a great moral help to me afterwards, and the excitement and adventure suited something in my nature. The background of battle sharpened my sensibility and heightened my visual perception. I vividly remember nights as this one about which I wrote home, 'It is a cloudy night, with a fierce cold wind. The moon and a few bright stars appear as they are uncovered here and there by the fast moving clouds. The guns ring out in sharp incisive tones. The crumps of the shells from both sides make the whole earth shiver and vibrate. Groups of men advance in the dark and are suddenly outlined by the various coloured lights that flare up at odd intervals. The whole world seems to be full of glorious uncertainty. There is something beautiful, something wonderful in the air!'

Different types of men reacted to the war in different ways. To most it was a frightening experience to be undergone, because of a high sense of duty and patriotism; and I sympathised with many who had reached almost the limit of endurance. I remember being isolated in a hospital tent with a few others, as it was thought we had caught diphtheria. When we were told we were free from infection, the man in the camp bed next to me was in despair at the thought of returning to the trenches. He would much have preferred the dangers of diphtheria!

To an inexperienced young man like myself the strange circumstances of the war aroused different sentiments. It made a deep appeal to emotions that would have remained dormant in ordinary civilian life. It created circumstances that made possible self-sacrifice for an ideal in the spirit of exaltation of a crusader. Here was a cause which demanded the greatest dedication with no personal advantage. It was my aim never to fail in the standard I had set for myself, as the completely fearless soldier. In all wars young men have been inspired by similar ambitions.

I had worked out that with so many chances of being hit, the risk was no greater if one took no protective precautions. It was purely a question of luck and I believed in my star. I remember I was so foolhardy that, on an occasion when having to reconnoitre our front line during heavy enemy shelling, I took my walking-stick and walked down a slope 'over the top', instead of in the trenches chock-full of casualties; and walked there and back in full view. This was not bravery; by acting in this way I banished fear. I even got a mention in dispatches for the incident, which we considered at the time an insult to the front-line soldier, for the red and gold-tabbed staff all got mentions several times a year whilst eating comfortably in their rear châteaux, far from the range of shell-fire. We held them in the deepest contempt.

Some time later I was on loan to the 127th Battery from my own battery, the 126th, positioned on the reverse side of a hill a quarter of a mile away. They had dug an enormous hole in which they had intended to build a large dugout with logs, sandbags and earth. Suddenly, the position of my former unit was spotted, and shells fell round it. Everyone ran for shelter into this big open excavation. It was impossible to stand still watching my own battery being shelled, so I strolled over to join them. I was met with shouts of 'you bloody fool', so I pretended I had come to borrow a bottle of whisky. I stayed until the shelling was over and no shell, thank God, hit us.

I had flu' going home on my first leave, having got frozen on a long journey in an open cattle-truck, and was given an

extra fortnight's leave. But I went back with that extra leave
in my pocket. One week of London's night life, amidst the
luxury and apparent indifference to the war effort of the
population at home, was enough for me. It seemed a cleans-
ing process to be back with my battery again. And I had
heard that the second battle of the Somme was to start. I did
not want to miss it.

For quite a long period of the war the right wing of my
division (the 4th) rested on the River Scarpe, running from
west to east from the town of Arras. We held the crest of the
Point du Jour, a hill we captured at the same time as the
Canadians took the Vimy ridge on our left. From the top of
the ridge one could see for miles behind the enemy lines; our
own front line was a mile lower down.

During a period in this part of the front an extraordinary
coincidence occurred. It was a beautiful summer's day. The
battery was firing away full-blast and there was excitement
in the air, such as occurs in the opening days of a new
offensive. As a company of the 1st Battalion of the Rifle
Brigade came marching through our gun positions, I suddenly saw my cousin Alfred Schiff at the head of his platoon. I
rushed to shake his hand and could hardly believe that out of
the blue, on his first day in the line, he should just come
through my own battery. I told him I would look him up
that evening, as I would be acting as F.O.O. at his battalion
headquarters.

Alfred was under-officer at Sandhurst when I was under-
officer at Woolwich, and he was the only nephew of my
Uncle Sydney. We had spent many happy holidays together.

Alas, that night he was sent out on a routine patrol and
did not return. With one of the corporals of his platoon I
went out to search for him, crawling about no-man's-land in
the early hours of the morning under sporadic bursts of
machine-gun fire, until we found him two hundred yards
beyond our wire. He had been killed instantly. I suddenly
recalled the many confidences we had exchanged, his father

and sister who adored him, and his light-hearted mood of the previous day; and I had to leave him unburied in a wet and lonely shell-hole! It was a terrible moment.

How strange is fate that strikes one man down on the first day of battle and leaves another unharmed for years. A similar experience happened to me twenty years later. I had returned from Dunkirk and my young partner, David (Lord Long), was bemoaning that I had been through the Dunkirk campaign and he, a captain in the Coldstream, had not yet seen a shot fired in battle. When we went back to France he was killed by a sniper the first day he landed in Normandy. Going into battle, even with the knowledge that large casualties are inevitable, each individual believes he will be the lucky one and escape unharmed. An old hand may get through and the latest arrival be the first casualty; it is a pure lottery.

My best friend in the battery was Colin Gubbins,[1] a year older than I, who had been out in France since 1914, when he left the Shop. Small, good-looking, with a little black moustache, he is one of the bravest men I have ever met. He used to induce me to go out at night with him, sniping between the lines and doing other foolish things in a mood of youthful recklessness and enjoyment.

Our major, Robert Staveley, held himself rather aloof from his junior officers, and we still called him 'Sir' after two years serving together in the same battery. He was the type of efficient, though rather unimaginative, regular officer who had served in India. I remember an episode when he was haranguing the men before a particularly hazardous operation. I had quite recently been F.O.O. with a French battalion, and had been on more than friendly terms with them as I spoke French fluently. In similar circumstances the French commandant would have trotted out words like *La France, La Patrie, L'Honneur*, etc. Staveley, after outlining the details of the next morning's attack, just said 'Well,

[1] Now Major-General Sir Colin Gubbins, K.C.M.G., D.S.O., M.C.

that's the job, you're big and ugly enough to carry it out'.

Many of my real friends were amongst the signallers. The kind of work we had to do attracted a particular Cockney type. Slum dwellers, they had been unable to adjust themselves to the dreary working-class conditions of the time; and their adventurous spirit had on occasion brought them before the local police court. They might have been considered misfits in the slums at home; but not out here on the Western Front. No wounded man of the 'team' would ever be left behind. The old d'Artagnan motto of 'one for all and all for one' was never better applied than to my little group. Going 'over the top' with the F.O.O. and the infantry was a normal military experience, as everyone was together. But it was quite another thing to go out alone mending a long telephone-line on a dark and rainy night during a heavy bombardment.

I enjoyed the company of these men, learning the stories of their lives, gradually brought out during long waits in dugouts, whilst drinking the strongest black witches' brew, army tea. Their language was spontaneous Cockney humour, inspired by the moment and the peculiarities of the individual concerned. I remember one day in a dugout during a particularly unpleasant bombardment near Ypres, being afraid to go to sleep for fear of gas-shells. These exuded a very sweet smell, which made one want to breathe it in. 'It's all right', said one of them; 'Fred's on duty and 'e's got a nose like an 'awk.' I was completely convinced and immediately dropped off to sleep.

The front-line soldiers' contempt for the Staff and British generalship reached its height during the Passchendaele campaign. Anyone with the slightest knowledge of the country should have known that the water was only a yard or two below the surface of the vast plains over which we were to attack. Naturally enough, our bombardment caused deep pools through which the attacking troops had to wade.

It was not possible to dig dugouts, so the only available shelters were the occasional captured German concrete pill-boxes.

We kept only skeleton crews with the guns, and our casualties at the gun emplacements for a time were as high as 25 per cent a week. Often the safest place was the front line, when its exact position was unknown by either side, and so, immune from shell-fire. Colin and I had many strange adventures when trying to locate our forward positions.

On one occasion we had to sink ourselves up to the neck in water to escape the machine-gun bullets of a solitary enemy aeroplane flying at low altitude. On another we had to lie down without moving until dark, near some very unpleasant German corpses, having been about to enter what we thought was a deserted pill-box, now occupied by the enemy.

Our battery headquarters were once in the famous Menin Gate, a part of the old fortifications of Ypres, built by Vauban for Louis XIV: the system of heavy earthworks held together by stout walls was well able to withstand the test of modern bombardment. Whilst at dinner in our mess at the Menin Gate, the old seventeenth-century guard-room, we could listen to the bombardment with equanimity. A direct hit at most put out the candles. In the wide moat outside, the beautiful white swans glided about, undisturbed by the noise of our firing guns or the falling shells.

But despite everything we had our lighthearted moments. Whenever I was back at the wagon-lines, usually some three miles behind the front, I used to go for runs to keep fit. On one occasion the routine Corps orders, generally used as lavatory paper, commanded all ranks to carry tin-hats and gas-masks continuously. To the hilarious approval of all, I was ordered to wear my tin-hat and gas-mask whilst going for a run in shorts.

During occasional spells behind the lines, the regiment got great amusement out of organising theatricals. My nickname B.B. was a gift to the comic cards! One of the sergeants could never resist singing that very popular song of the moment:

> I'm Burlington Bertie,
> I rise at ten-thirty,
> And go for a stroll in the Park

amid the cat-calls of all my battery.

Walter had gone to the front a couple of months before I did. We were never allowed to belong to the same unit as army regulations prevented brothers serving together. He was in the 51st Division and I only saw him for a few moments once at the front, though we wrote to each other constantly. Then I got the news that he had been killed at Hellfire Corner, near Ypres, bringing up ammunition to his guns for the Passchendaele offensive. He was only nineteen and had been a whole year in the line.

It was a terrible blow, and I was specially overwhelmed with remorse, because during his last leave he had behaved rather foolishly (or shall I say naturally) over a girl he was in love with, and had run into debt. I had sent him some cash, but with a rather reprimanding letter. And this only a week before he was killed. I could not forgive myself for my self-righteous attitude.

I have often thought that if you have loved somebody who has died, it seems possible to inherit some of their qualities, if only through thinking about them so much, and about those traits of character so deeply admired and loved.

I never used to sing before Walter died, but later I took up singing and worked at it all my life with an ardent desire to improve my performance. Of course, I could never emulate Walter's marvellous voice, but I feel in a way that from him I have inherited the pleasure of singing. Almost every day I have begun the morning by practising my songs. It has given me great enjoyment and a feeling of detachment and serenity, which has protected me from changes of fortune and periods of unhappiness. I always feel that this is a gift bestowed on me by my memory of him.

When I had been continuously on the Western Front for over two years my enthusiasm was in no way dimmed by all I had gone through. As I said before, I felt protected by a fatalistic approach to death, so danger itself was not to be feared. I had also learned to train myself for this continuous ordeal. I never drank, because it was Colin's (and my own) experience, without any exception, that no officer could survive more than one year in the trenches, unless he was abstemious in his drinking habits. Of course, I do not mean a puritanical abstinence, such as not joining in a gay party or having a good tot of rum or whisky on a cold night in the trenches. But as soon as a man started to take to the bottle to drown his fears, he was doomed. His fears were multiplied after each attack and his morale gradually disintegrated. I found that living for months at a stretch in trenches or dugouts required a strict personal discipline, and I therefore took a lot of trouble to keep myself neat and clean. I had a light rubber bath and it was generally set up in a shell-hole, the water being heated in an old petrol tin.

Early in 1918 the Germans staged a masterly counter-offensive against the Fifth Army, with devastating effect. My division was the right division of the Third Army, and we were back in our old position on the Point du Jour ridge. The River Scarpe on our right was the dividing line between us and the Fifth Army, which was in mass retreat.

The troops on our front had been thinned out, to give reinforcement to the Fifth Army, and we were daily expecting an all-out offensive, as Intelligence reported an enormous increase in reinforcements of enemy troops opposite our lines.

I went to Battalion H.Q. as F.O.O. one night with considerable apprehension, taking with me the pick of my telephone gang. The H.Q. was about 250 yards behind the front line, and as I manned the parapet of our trench just before dawn, I saw a sight I will never forget.

The sun had not yet risen, but its first red glow had suddenly struck the line of bayonets on the parapet of the German trenches, stretching from right to left before me in an irregular shape. Ready for the attack, the German infantry were holding their rifles beside them on the parapet, only the bayonets protruding above the trench. There was something appallingly beautiful in the sight of that long pink line of steel gleaming in the early dawn.

And then came the overwhelming bombardment. Standing beside the battalion commander, I was on the telephone to the company commander immediately in front. His last heroic message was: 'The Germans have just reached the wire. We will do the best we can.'

Afterwards everything was smoke, dust, exploding shells and confusion. But somehow retreating down a communication trench, we managed to get hold of a machine-gun whose team had been killed, and we kept the gun going, sweeping down the hill continuously over a wide arc. At the time we thought everyone was still around us and we were not aware, till we were told later, that this solitary machine-gun had held up the attack at a critical moment, as our front line had been overwhelmed. In the feverish excitement and confusion, I had only seized the weapon in a kind of desperation. When our ammunition had run out, we retired to our telephone-line, managed to mend it and got it working again.

That day I felt frightened in a way I had never been before. Of course, I had experienced fear on numerous occasions, but had managed to overcome it. Now only my will-power kept me going.

It was a day of unexpected happenings. I saw a German battery, with its horses, unlimber its guns in the valley just opposite our old front line. Within minutes I got my battery trained on this target. For the first time in the war I had

c

engaged enemy guns manœuvring in the open. The German
artillery were, no doubt, advancing to a timetable, but our
infantry, who had been reinforced, had held their positions
half-way up the Point du Jour ridge.

My anxiety was to continue to man our telephone communications, and new volunteers took the place of those
who had become casualties.

Later a surprising event occurred. Instead of the battery
retreating, as we had expected, there was Colin advancing
with all six guns, the horse teams going forward at full
gallop, to the top of the Point du Jour ridge, to fire with
open sights at the enemy, in support of our infantry. It
looked like a picture of an old-fashioned battle.

I am not clear what happened after that. Colin was
wounded. My dugout got a direct hit. I was miraculously
saved by a heavy beam which held the earth above me, but
the remainder of my signallers were killed. I was dragged
out, suffering from gas and shock, put on a stretcher and
sent down to a Casualty Clearing Station, situated in a
deserted railway station. I lay there, breathing heavily from
phosgene gas and utterly exhausted. The rumour came that
the Germans were about to capture the station, and many of
the wounded picked up their stretchers and walked away. But
I no longer cared.

Suddenly, an Australian ambulance train puffed into the
station. It was one of the most heavenly moments of my life.
Feminine hands lifted me into a soft bunk; charming voices
were solicitous of every comfort. I had so often dreamed on
lonely nights of just such an experience; and now this
wonderful dream had come true.

Whilst crossing the Channel I noticed a tag on my
stretcher, 'No. 3 General Hospital'. I crossed it out and put
instead the name of Lady Carnarvon, whom I knew, who
had, I had heard, turned her town house into a hospital. My
subterfuge worked. As I got better, pretty nurses accompanied me to night-clubs to revive my morale, which was

rather low at the time, for one result of my shell-shock was that I suddenly became bald. This was quite a blow to my vanity and for years made me look older than my age. Whilst in hospital I was notified of my Bar to the Military Cross.

On convalescent leave I enjoyed my first London 'season'. Dances at that time were given in large London houses, not in hotels. All the young people were introduced by the hostess, so you had the excitement of hoping that perhaps at that very dance you would meet 'the only girl in the world'. And, of course, young men were expected to look out for the wall-flowers and invite them to dance as well.

It was smart in a certain social set for officers not to wear uniform. Going to parties meant putting on a white tie, as you could not be seen with a lady while wearing a smoking-jacket.

Lord Herbert Scott's charming nieces took me under their wing and introduced me to their very lively circle. The eldest, Mida,[1] had been nursing in France and I had been to visit her several times at her base hospital when on short leave from the front. The younger one, Sybil,[2] was just coming out.

I was invited to Langholm, the Buccleuch shooting-box in Scotland. The duke, who owned numerous castles, entertained in great style a few weeks at a time at each of his different residences. I remember a particularly thoughtful act of his when I arrived. It was a very long drive from the station, and he insisted on giving me a golden sovereign, the exact fare, adding that young subalterns couldn't afford such expensive taxi-rides. He said it so kindly that I accepted with gratitude.

I am afraid I disgraced myself the first evening in front of a house party of some thirty guests. Accustomed for so long to sitting on boxes of ammunition, I leaned back carelessly and broke a beautiful Sheraton chair. 'Don't give it a

[1] Now Lady Margaret Hawkins.   [2] Now Lady Sybil Phipps.

thought,' said the duke; 'we've got plenty of chairs.' But some of the older guests looked at me with marked disapproval.

Shooting parties were organised every day, the girls never taking part, but following and helping with the picnic lunch. It seemed so strange after two years in the trenches to meet tall, bearded Lord Edward Manners, who spent his life going from one shoot to another, as if nothing else mattered in life. My shooting, after all my experience at the front, was atrocious.

It was a wonderful holiday. The Scott family, including the two younger sisters, Mary[1] and Alice,[2] published a little illustrated magazine, to which I contributed. They used to call me 'Edwardski', it being the fashion to add Russian endings to names as a gesture to our Russian allies.

Back in London, I made up my mind to return to the front as soon as possible. I wanted to prove to myself that I had not lost my nerve. My first medical board turned me down flat. But I managed to wangle an appearance before a different one who agreed to my request.

Leaving England, I wrote home, 'It is just getting dark. I am on board with a battalion of the Grenadier Guards, whom we saw at Charing Cross with the bands playing. They are fine-looking fellows. The sun is setting and clouds form a multi-coloured pattern in the sky. Everyone has gone on deck to have a last look at dear old England, which we will not see again before passing through many strange experiences. The light is fading and the soldiers are singing their quaint and funny songs, ranging from sentimental to ragtime. Very rough, perhaps, if heard in a concert hall, but beautifully in harmony with the general calmness of the sea and clouds and our feelings at the moment.'

I was appointed captain to one of the new army artillery regiments, and arrived in the midst of a fierce battle, where

[1] Later Lady Burghley.   [2] Now the Duchess of Gloucester.

my regiment had had heavy casualties. The Germans, retreating on their large ammunition dumps, had unlimited ammunition and were able to launch successful counter-attacks on our over-extended line.

To my astonishment my new battery commander was my former company commander at the Shop, who had been quite a hero to us then and had done so much to inspire us with the high ideals of the Regular officer. He was in a state of near collapse and had retreated, leaving the wounded behind. The battery, which seemed a rather undisciplined lot, were in a state of sullen semi-revolt. This officer had been kept back at the Shop for four years because he was such an inspiring teacher. But however efficient an officer may appear under peacetime conditions, the final test is in battle. And you can never tell beforehand how the test will be faced. Here was an unhappy example of this, a man who was unable to measure up to the standard he had set himself and his cadets in the past. The situation was a dangerous one for his future career, for he might have been court-martialled. The regimental doctor saved the day by having him evacuated as a shell-shock case. I felt very sorry for him.

The regiments of the new armies had long since reached and surpassed the former standard of the Regular Army, for they had the élite of the nation to draw on. But after four years of war and enormous casualties, reinforcements were being sent to the front without adequate training, let alone experience. The battery, which was part of a newly-created regiment, was mostly made up of these miscellaneous reinforcements. Its large casualties when first going into action, and the collapse of its commander, had had a bad moral effect all round.

Because of my long battle experience, I was promoted to the rank of major in command of the battery, with the order to lick my command into shape.

As I was only twenty-one myself and younger than any N.C.Os., I had to establish unquestionable leadership over both the officers and the battery as a whole. This required a demonstration of ruthlessness on my part at first, which however would not have been effective unless tempered by generous appreciation and cordiality as soon as conditions improved.

The battery behaved splendidly in our last advance through the former battlefields to the German frontier. But I no longer had the feeling of fearlessness as in former years, being unable to throw off the effect of my recent shell-shock. I tried by taking unnecessary risks to prove to myself that I was the same man as before, but in reality I was in a state of constant apprehension and suffered from bad insomnia. Only my will-power kept me going, though the exercise of this will-power became more and more self-destructive. Fortunately, six weeks after my return to France the armistice was declared.

I was immediately demoted from major to captain (lieutenant temporary captain) and a major who had spent the whole war in Ireland took over the battery! Never was anyone more disliked by the men.

With the armistice there arose a bad feeling in the army. Everyone wanted to go home, and the new 'dugouts' who had come out as officer reinforcements to take over senior positions were not appreciated by the front-line troops.

One day our new colonel, who was almost permanently drunk, invited some French prostitutes to the mess, and allowed the mess servants to serve them at dinner. Enraged by this, I got hold of my King's Regulations and having studied them very carefully, put my colonel under arrest for being drunk and for 'conduct prejudicial to military discipline'. This caused a considerable stir in higher military circles, but fortified by King's Regulations I held my ground. When the great day came for the court-martial, the brigadier acting as president or judge did not wait to hear the evidence. 'What's the charge?' 'Drunk!' 'Why shouldn't he be drunk? Case dismissed!' And that was that. My first attempt at social reform had fallen flat. Had the accused been a Sergeant Major he would have been demoted to the ranks, and forfeited most of his long-earned pension.

Soon afterwards I received a reply to my application to go to the Staff College. The answer was that I could not qualify for entry until I was thirty, so I decided to leave the army as soon as possible.

Chapter Two

★

OXFORD

THEN came a change of fortune due to fortuitous circumstances. This was a pattern often to be repeated in my life in future years. I am a believer in the idea that opportunity comes to one like a train entering a station; and one must seize it and jump on before the train moves off again. Also I believe that opportunity occurs in an unexpected way, often the more unpremeditated the greater the chance of success.

I had written a letter to the *New Statesman*, something about using the idealism that inspired the soldier during the war to build up a new, peaceful world. It was no doubt very naïve, but it resulted in a correspondence with Dr Thomas Strong, the Dean of Christ Church. This led to my going to Oxford in the winter term of 1919. I was still twenty-one.

Oxford, after four years as a soldier, was a most exciting experience. I felt so ignorant, and there was the whole world of knowledge suddenly open to me.

But I was a nervous wreck. I slept little and even a short walk exhausted me. Going back to the front to try and recover my nerve had had a disastrous effect. As physically I appeared quite normal, nobody seemed to sympathise with or understand my mental anguish. This made me feel that the world was against me.

Somebody suggested I should visit the local mental hospital specialising in cases resulting from the war. I knew nothing of psycho-analysis at the time, but I have an enquiring mind, and decided to investigate the treatment. So I came under the care of Dr Goode, the Principal.

The general idea of the treatment, of course, is that anxiety occurs because some incidents in one's life have not been rationally interpreted and this has resulted in a conflict between one's conscious and unconscious mind. Only by permitting the conscious mind to be aware of unconscious thoughts can the anxiety be removed.

The analysis of dreams, the quick association of words, if done by a skilled practitioner, reveal hidden anxieties or complexes in the subconscious. The conscious mind is then able gradually to adjust itself to reality.

It is important in such a treatment for the doctor not to suggest what is wrong to the patient, or what the particular dream or association means. This is what the bad psychiatrists do, with unhappy results, as the power of suggestion gradually diminishes and has no permanent effect. Whilst if the doctor helps the patient to work out his case for himself, no false diagnosis occurs and the cure is permanent.

This is what happened to me, thanks to the patience and wisdom of that truly remarkable Dr Goode.

In a few months I was fitter and more mentally alert than I had ever been before. In fact, the shell-shock, and the effort required to overcome its effects, had greatly heightened my sensibility and intellectual powers.

Through Dr Goode I learned how soldiers might be immunised against shell-shock before going into battle. They should be told that it is natural to feel frightened when shells and bullets are flying around, and this is not in any way ignoble. If they are able to give or receive orders, without showing outward signs of nervousness, they have mastered the situation. I remembered this advice, with good results, twenty years later in the Second World War!

Having got over the first effects of shell-shock, I threw myself with zest into the variety and excitement of Oxford life. I attended the debates of the Oxford Union, and joined and helped to start numerous Oxford societies. I remember one I formed with Lord De La Warr called the Massinni Society, whose motto was 'Duty before Privilege', or some such high-sounding principle. He had invited George Lansbury, the Labour leader and editor of the *Daily Herald* to a meeting. Lansbury was fêted and his sentimental speech warmly applauded by the undergraduates. He declared himself enchanted by his reception. However, to our astonishment, twenty-four hours later the *Daily Herald* published a scathing article by him about his visit, mentioning the De La Warr Rolls-Royce that brought him to Oxford and the bottles of champagne that flowed at his reception, giving the impression that champagne was the undergraduates' normal beverage.

Among the leading speakers at the Union who were my close friends were Hore-Belisha, Beverley Nichols, Edward Marjoribanks and Bob Boothby. Hore-Belisha was not really popular, though he well deserved his presidency of the Union for the brilliance of his oratory. He conducted the securing of votes on that occasion as in a Parliamentary campaign, inviting an incredible number of members to sumptuous breakfasts.

Beverley Nichols was an example of how outstanding talent often flares up in early youth: the very brilliance of the flame seeming to cause its early diminution. He has had a most successful career as a journalist and writer of popular fiction, but the quality of his speeches at the Union and the charm of his personality gave promise of much greater things to come; whilst Anthony Eden and Derick Heathcoat Amory, whom we all liked, never attracted particular attention at the time.

I read history, which then corresponded to the present-day P.P.E.: a mixture of history, political science and economics. My tutor, J. C. Masterman,[1] who later became Provost of Worcester and Vice-Chancellor of Oxford University, took

[1] Now Sir John Masterman.

infinite pains to encourage me in my studies, and I will always be grateful to him for his help in that critical period of my life. I took as a special subject French history from the French Revolution to the Battle of Waterloo, which meant reading up that period, not just from history books, but from original documents of the time, at the Ashmolean or the British Museum. I have since appreciated that one of the advantages of a university education is that you learn to do original research in your special subject. It teaches you a technique that can be applied in other directions. This early training has been most helpful to me in dealing with questions I have later wanted to examine: whether political or economic problems, business, archaeology or the breeding of pedigree cattle.

I was advised to take up running again, as a means of dispersing the remnants of phosgene gas. It suited me well, as I had so much work to do to make up for those lost years that I found it took less time to get fit by running than any other sport. Once you have got yourself properly trained, you can keep in racing condition by less than a quarter of an hour's running every day.

Before every race I used to have a feeling of intense nervous strain, and often swore to myself I would never race again. Lloyd George once told me that he made the best speeches when he felt most nervous beforehand. In my case, once the race started I enjoyed the excitement of competition and the feeling of extending myself to the uttermost. I often found myself beating someone who, in practice runs, did better times than I could, because I was more nervously strung up in an actual race.

I got my blue for the mile, though the half-mile was my distance. Being broad and six foot tall, I was not physically made to compete successfully as a first string at longer distances. But being an all-round runner I also took part in the Oxford team of eight, in the nine-mile cross-country races in the winter, since this did not interfere with my running shorter distances in the spring. In one of these races, after a gruelling struggle up a steep hill, I had been sick with four miles still to go; and I remember Schrubb, our trainer and a former British long-distance champion, running alongside and saying, 'Whatever happens, try to pass the four runners ahead of you in this ploughed field. If you can do so they will not attempt to overtake you later'. I struggled hard and, telling myself that I had only the ploughed field to cover, I just managed to get ahead of the four competitors. Schrubb had the right appreciation of the part that psychological mastery can play in physical contests; I ambled easily along afterwards to the end of the race and was not challenged again.

Rudd, our captain, was Olympic record-holder for the half-mile, and at that time was the only Englishman who beat me at that distance. He had a delightful personality and a splendid physique. He was one of the most popular men of my generation up at Oxford and seemed to fit in his championship achievements without the 'specialisation' imposed on modern athletes.

One day I got a letter from the young sister of a former officer friend, asking herself to lunch as she was going to visit a convent at Oxford, where she had been to school. I had only a vague remembrance of a silent schoolgirl from the rare occasions I had been to her brother's home. On a fine summer's morning there appeared a pretty pink-complexioned girl, whom I took out on the river, with a picnic lunch aboard. After a pleasant day together, during which we became quite friendly, I suggested it was time to go back to the convent. 'Oh no!' she said, 'I have no intention of going there. It was just an excuse. I came up to Oxford to run away with you.' Having heard so much about me from her brother, she had a schoolgirl crush on an imaginary person, which was me. My pleasure in meeting her and spending several hours lazily on the river suddenly evaporated. I had visions of marriage, or scandal and the unexpected break-up of my

Racing at Queen's Club, 1920

The author on Coronation, the winner of the
Heavyweight Hunter Class at Olympia, 1938

university life for the sake of someone I would not have recognised in the street the previous day. I hurriedly telephoned her mother, and put the tearful girl on the train back to London.

I was up for the shortened course, which enabled officers to take their degree in two years. The first year I lived in college, the second in 'digs'. Six of us took a delightful old house opposite Tom Quad, called Micklem Hall. This was an oak-panelled seventeenth-century house with a pleasant garden and a spare room. One of us was studying economics and he explained that everything would work out quite cheaply as our expenses would be divided by six. Henry Hope,[1] Philip Rea,[2] the Hon. Reggie Wynn and W. O. S. Moloney shared Micklem Hall with me. We had a dear old couple to look after us and we greatly enjoyed ourselves. But things did not quite work out as planned by our economic expert. All the bills were divided by six, but they were multiplied by the dozens of friends who enjoyed our generous hospitality. At that time Oxford tradesmen encouraged undergraduates to run up large bills, knowing that their families were in a position to pay. I thus found myself in debt for the first time in my life. I sold my books and other possessions to get ready cash and also had to ask my father's help. Fortunately he responded generously. This incident had a profound effect, for since then I have never run into debt and have accustomed myself to pay all bills promptly.

The 'Varsity' then was quite different from Oxford University today. The undergraduates were mostly sons of well-off families, representing the ruling classes of that time, and I believe the standard of learning of the leading scholars was as high as it has ever been since. In my first year I had splendid oak-panelled rooms in Peckwater Quad, a bedroom, a spare room I used as a study and a large sitting-room. One rarely ate in restaurants in the town, as the food at the

[1] Now Lord Rankeillour.   [2] Now Lord Rea.

'House' (Christ Church) was both cheaper and much better than could be obtained anywhere in Oxford. Food was not expensive in those days, and the House prided itself on a very fine 'cuisine'. Its meringues were reputed to be second to none and the usual picnic lunch provided for punting on the river consisted of cold salmon, cold chicken, and strawberries and cream. We therefore had all our meals in our rooms, except for dinner in Hall. The 'scouts' carried our food on their heads, sometimes for long distances — across the quadrangles, from the central kitchen near the Hall.

It was the custom for the scouts to be remunerated partly in the form of 'perquisites'. This meant that more food was ordered by them than was actually required by the undergraduates; the remainder being taken home for their families. I felt this system to be quite wrong. I thought the scouts should receive a proper living wage and not be put in the position of having to behave dishonestly.

I went to see the Dean about it. He was patient and sympathetic, as he had been before when I had suggested that it was unsuitable for some of the Christ Church income to be derived from the slums on the outskirts of Oxford. He obviously realised that this strange breed of war-time ex-officer would soon be replaced by a more normal undergraduate generation.

Some time later a deputation of scouts asked if they could see me. I imagined it was to thank me for my efforts on their behalf. Six scouts turned up, and the eldest one, about three times my own age, read out the following declaration, written in the most beautiful script, which they afterwards presented to me. 'We, the scouts of Christ Church, conscious of our duties towards the undergraduates of the college, do hereby declare that the system of perquisites, which has continued for generations, is a symbol of the undergraduates' appreciation of the services given by the scouts, and the scouts' high esteem and devotion to the undergraduates they are happy to serve. We consider that any change in this system would destroy one of the oldest and most cherished college traditions.'

My reforming spirit had met the same kind of response as when I had put my colonel under arrest!

On the first armistice anniversary I helped to organise a college rag and, as the senior ex-officer, I was appointed master of ceremonies. We had a large dinner at which many toasts were drunk. I suggested we should give a gunnery display for the benefit of the City of Oxford.

At that time it was the fashion for enemy guns to be given to institutions as trophies. Magdalen had two enormous German 150-millimetre howitzers. There was a friendly rivalry between Magdalen and Christ Church. Occasionally one college would untie all the punts of the other, just before Eights week, encouraging them to drift down the river.

I called for ex-gunner volunteers and amid great hilarity we dragged these giant guns from Magdalen down the High, down St Aldate's, and pushed them over Folly Bridge into the Isis. I almost went over with them.

It was a tumultuous occasion, but the guns held up the river traffic and it took a week to remove them with heavy cranes. Once again the Dean showed a high sense of political tact, and I escaped being sent down.

I had many close friends in the House; some of them like Prince Paul of Jugoslavia and Roy Harrod[1] are intimate friends today. Others I got to know better later on, like Ronald Howe, later to become head of Scotland Yard, and Fred Warburg, now an eminent publisher.

It was through my friend Victor Cazalet[2] that I bought my first picture. I had seen a wonderful head by Picasso at the Rosenberg Gallery in Paris, and had said to myself that I would give anything to buy that picture if only I had the money. It happened that twenty-four hours later Victor and

[1] Now Sir Roy Harrod.
[2] Victor Cazalet, M.P., was killed in an aeroplane accident with General Sikorski in 1942.

I and other friends were celebrating New Year's Eve at the Palace Hotel, St Moritz. Knowing that any wine immediately went to my head, Victor plied me with champagne, and at a critical moment said to me, 'I challenge you to go into the baccarat room and put a doll on the table and say "Banco"!' The stakes were high in the baccarat room and I had neither the means nor the inclination to gamble. But I took up the challenge, and because I was ignorant of the game and in a dazed mental state at the time, money accumulated in front of me; and I soon found I had some £500 in Swiss francs. Hardly able to believe my luck, I paid my hotel bill, went straight to Paris next day and bought the Picasso from Rosenberg for £380.

I saw a lot of the Sitwells at that time. Sacheverell was up at the House, and his sister, Edith, and his elder brother, Osbert, lived together at Oxford, as did their composer friend Willie Walton.[1] Sydney Schiff knew them very well They were the centre of a very interesting intellectual circle. The three Sitwells always stuck together, and any criticism of one of them, even if legitimate literary comment, led to a permanent quarrel with them all. My subsequent friendship with Wyndham Lewis, with whom they eventually quarrelled, unfortunately caused a coolness in our relations. Funnily enough, twenty years later I was to donate my portrait of Edith Sitwell by Wyndham Lewis to the Tate Gallery.

I was very much interested in politics but could not decide to which party to give my allegiance. I particularly liked Jimmie Maxton, the leader of the Independent Labour Party, one of the most attractive and warm-hearted idealists I had ever met; and my visits to centres of unemployment filled me with deep shame. But the Labour Party seemed to me most intolerant at the time and its factions so bitter. I had more friends in Conservative circles, but their policies appeared to me too selfish and devoid of constructive effort

[1] Sir William Walton.

As an undergraduate, I purchased my first picture — a Picasso, 1920

Author, League of Nations, 1921

in dealing with unemployment and social reform. Through Philip Rea's father, and visits to Sutton Courtenay where Lord Oxford held court, I was also in close touch with the Liberal Party, but its fratricidal warfare was upsetting. I remember a public meeting at Oxford when, after Sir John Simon had spoken in eloquent terms of Lord Oxford, the principal speaker, Lady Oxford, who hated Simon, ex-claimed aloud for all to hear, 'What a rotten speech!'

One of the most fascinating men I met up at Oxford was Father Martindale, head of the Jesuit College. He was immensely popular with my generation of undergraduates and never intruded religious subjects unless asked to do so. He was brilliantly clever, and we all enjoyed discussing even the most controversial subjects with him, for he was always open-minded and well-informed. Those of us who had personal problems would find in him a ready listener and sympathetic adviser. I have kept up my friendship with him ever since. He was in Denmark during the Second World War, and imprisoned by the Germans when they invaded the country, as the Nazis hated the Jesuits for their opposition to their racial policies. When I saw him again soon after his return to England, he was terribly emaciated from his privations. He is now over 80, but managed to write me a little note this Christmas, saying he was having blood-transfusions, and sending me greetings.

D

Chapter Three

★

LEAGUE OF NATIONS

I GOT my degree, but had no definite idea as to what to take up as a future career, except that eventually I wanted to go into politics. It never occurred to me to consider business, and such was the attitude of mind in my undergraduate circle that I rather pitied a cousin of mine, destined to go into his father's bank!

As a preliminary training for politics I put myself down for a Foreign Office examination. But fate decided otherwise. I had intended to run in some relay-races against Harvard and Yale, but hurt my ankle while practising the quarter-mile hurdles. As I was unable to run that weekend, I accepted my tutor's suggestion to go in for an examination for entry to the newly-created Secretariat of the League of Nations, which would be good practice for my Foreign Office examination later.

To my surprise I came first in this test and, as a result, was offered a post in the International Labour Office of the League of Nations in Geneva. The salary was £850, free of tax, which in those days had the purchasing power of £3,000 a year tax-free today. Had I not hurt my ankle I would never have considered taking the exam.

I was delighted at the idea of this job which, besides offering me the prospect of a fascinating new experience, fell into line with the principle in which I believed; to take advantage of unpremeditated opportunities.

The object of the International Labour Office (I.L.O.)

was to bring about the levelling up of labour legislation, and generally to improve conditions of labour throughout the world. Because of the dominating and creative personality of its director, Albert Thomas, who had been Minister of Munitions in the French government, the I.L.O. was a much more dynamic organisation than its parent body, the League of Nations, which was under the direction of Sir Eric Drummond, later Lord Perth, a typically cautious Foreign Office official.

My work on the League of Nations was most stimulating. I had intimate contact with the leading political figures of the moment who came to Geneva, at that time the world's political forum.

During conferences there was no simultaneous translation of speeches transmitted through earphones, as at present. When a speaker had finished, the translator got up and summarised his speech in English and French, the two official languages. By chance, one day I was asked to take a translator's place, and so discovered I had an aptitude for this type of work. I would put down headings quickly in a notebook, then get up and make the speech, skipping repetitions, so that sometimes the translated speech was almost better than the original and actually got rounds of applause. In this way I translated speeches of Barthou, and other leading continental statesmen, and came to appreciate their various styles of oratory. My principal work, however, was in the political section under Edward Phelan.

Edward Phelan is an Irishman of originality and genius. Before the First World War he had been travelling about Europe, leading Cook's tours. When war came he was a temporary civil servant in the Ministry of Labour. At the time of the creation of the League of Nations there was a vague idea that a Labour Section was needed to canalise the growing demand for social reform along constructive lines, but no one had any precise idea how it should be done until, out of the blue, Phelan produced a draft of a complete constitution and proposed aims of the International Labour Office. It was adopted, almost without amendment, and has stood the test of over forty years. Though the League of Nations eventually collapsed and the United Nations took its place, the I.L.O. is still doing constructive work today. Phelan's great contribution was the idea that all its committees and activities should be controlled, half by government delegates and half by an equal number of representatives of trade-union and employers' organisations.

When I first joined the League of Nations I was twenty-three and very much in love with Joanna, the beautiful sister of one of my college friends, who came to Geneva with her parents. The whole family was victimised by the mother who, though most charming, was always in a highly nervous state. She dominated them by her strong personality and they were forced to placate her 'nerves'. Joanna, with her unselfish nature, was the chief sufferer, and I longed to rescue and comfort her. I eventually asked her to marry me, but was refused. I was most unhappy at that time, but later realised that the marriage would not have worked out happily for either of us, for my feelings for her were largely founded on compassion, which is the wrong basis for married life. Unfortunately, it has often happened to me: to fall in love and suffer disappointment.

My most intimate friends on the League were Phelan, Harold Butler (deputy director of the I.L.O.) and Philip Noel-Baker, who was deputy to Sir Eric Drummond. I saw a good deal of Jean Monnet, whom I was to meet so often in later years. I also made friends with Lord Robert Cecil and Professor Gilbert Murray, who were constantly in Geneva as leaders of the League of Nations Union. Gilbert Murray, perhaps the greatest of Greek scholars, had been most kind to me when I was up at Oxford, and I admired his noble character and generous nature.

Lord Robert Cecil, whose beak-like nose, prominent Adam's apple, and soiled, frayed butterfly-collar, gave him a peculiarly ascetic appearance, had certain characteristics that I subsequently observed in other political personalities whom I got to know, such as Philip Kerr (afterwards Lord Lothian) and Philip Noel-Baker himself. Lord Robert had lofty ideals and great intellectual powers, but he always wanted to be on the side of the angels, and lacked the measure of ruthlessness and pliability necessary for political leadership. He was too much a prophet in the wilderness and not enough a man of action, ever to bring about the realisation of the policies he so ardently advocated.

Soon after I went to Geneva, Father died suddenly of pleurisy in the South of France. He had led an active business life, as well as having participated in Chambers of Commerce and similar public activities. At sixty-three he had been persuaded to retire and enjoy a quiet life. After a year of inactivity he died of boredom at the first illness. I am sure this often happens. Sir Winston Churchill once said to me, 'The only way to relax and have a holiday is to work equally hard at something else.' He is certainly a splendid example of this maxim.

I was left with a modest inheritance. Like many able business-men Father was not experienced in matters of investment and, when he retired, had converted his good pound sterling currency into French francs, which had had a catastrophic fall in value.

Father and I were never really on intimate terms. He did not understand me, nor ever seem to want to know what I was thinking or feeling. After Walter was killed I shuddered when I heard him telling somebody, 'I gave my son to my country', as if he himself had performed an act of heroism or sacrifice. Our relationship was impersonal. When we had been separated for some time we were happy to see each other again, but after the first exchange of affectionate greetings, there was little we had to say that was of interest to either.

Remembering my relationship with my father, I have tried

my best to create a bond of trust with my own son, Serge. When he was a child I always tried to spend some time alone with him every day, without his mother or the nurse being present. And ever since I have taken great pains to establish a basis of real friendship between us.

My League of Nations work involved living partly in Geneva and partly in London. Some of the work of the London office included propaganda, and I learnt a good lesson in propaganda from the following incident. We used to send out the usual boring official communiqués, which had only a very limited newspaper coverage. One day my secretary mentioned that one of the girls on the Secretariat had won a prize for the fastest shorthand number of words a minute. I sent this information to the Press and it got world coverage and the widest publicity. This was a human story that interested people everywhere.

Through Frank Hodges, secretary of the British Mine-workers' Federation, I made a brief survey during one of my holidays of conditions in the South Wales coal industry. What a contrast to conditions today! Writing at the time I noted: 'Not to have seen the Rhondda Valley is not to have known what hell can be on earth. Imagine narrow valleys from eight to twelve miles long surrounded by high desolate uncultivated hills, without a house or a single tree, the sameness of their contours rendered more barren by a succession of monotonous, grey slag-heaps. In the valley a main thoroughfare with a tram-line, with one miserable row of houses either side, where the miners live. On each side of this road smoking pitheads and railway-lines; the whole shrouded in an atmosphere of smoke and drabness, which is brought into even more prominence by the shoddy cinema posters on the corners of the public-houses. Everywhere the buildings are that dull grey colour of the granite slag. No sight to relieve the eye of this monotony or deter the attention from the contemplation of oppressive misery.

'The streets and trams are full of miners — ragged black-faced, red-lipped men. There is hardly a mine in South Wales possessing baths; the darkness of the mine is brought back to the dingy home. Most of the miners I saw whose faces were not covered by thick, black, oily soot had that white, pasty complexion I had noticed in France among men who had spent too long underground in the dark atmosphere of a dugout.

'This is the part of South Wales that shelters the extremist element. It is no wonder that hardness and bitterness enters the soul of man, under such provoking and overwhelming circumstances.

'Yet, walking over the hills with a young trade-union official, I could not help noticing his love of the local barren hills and surroundings and his desire to remain there. This was the same kind of feeling I had encountered in mountain peasants, who would rather cultivate their barren rocky soil than leave to seek the easier life of the plains.'

Besides dealing with League problems at home, my work involved a good deal of travelling, representing the League at other international conferences on the Continent, or going to other countries overseas on official business. One of the journeys I remember best was my first visit to America at the end of 1922, with Albert Thomas, Edward Phelan and Paul Devinat,[1] a Frenchman on the Secretariat. The object of the journey was to acquaint the United States and Canada with the problems of the I.L.O. and the League of Nations, besides which, as a potential future French politician, Albert Thomas wanted to explore the possibilities of active financial help to the Allied countries.

Albert Thomas was a statesman on the highest level, a moving orator, an indefatigable worker. Had he not died a few years later, he would have made a great French Prime Minister, for France has always been reinvigorated by the

[1] Now a member of the French parliament, and several times a minister.

energetic leadership of men like Thomas, Poincaré, and Clemenceau, drawn from provincial families of modest means, and able to infuse the staunch qualities of peasant stock into French political life.

One of Thomas' most ardent hopes was to bring about a permanent French-German reconciliation, and to shape allied policy to this end. Had this policy succeeded, neither Hitler nor the Second World War might have occurred.

It was about Christmas time when we went to the United States, and we were warned that it might be extremely cold. I at first considered wearing Father's old fur-lined coat, but realising I would have to meet American labour leaders, as well as politicians, bankers and industrialists, I bought a heavy tweed coat instead. What was my surprise, when we were welcomed on our arrival at the New York docks by Samuel Gompers, president of the American Federation of Labour, to see him wearing the most sumptuous mink-lined fur coat. My astonishment was even greater when, on our first evening, he entertained us in great style at his magnificent flat in Park Avenue. I still had much to learn!

On the boat and during our long train journeys across America, the Thomas team had to work hard. We each made studies of political questions, which would be the subject of his speeches. One of my tasks was to read through the orations of Abraham Lincoln and other American statesmen, and note appropriate phrases which might come in useful. Having prepared the material, it was discussed amongst us and a general policy decided upon. When new factors arose in the situation, suitable changes were agreed on at the last moment.

In New York we met leading bankers like J. P. Morgan, Thomas Lamont and Otto Kahn. Leading members of the government received us in Washington and we were again surprised that, contrary to men in similar positions in Europe, they all appeared immensely wealthy, however modest their origins. We stayed for a week in Washington with Mr H. Hoover, at that time Secretary of Commerce and subsequently President of the United States. Throughout the day Hoover continually received ticker-tapes showing the latest share transactions on the stock-market. In my ignorance of Stock Exchange speculation at that time, I innocently asked the reason for the continued flow of details of Stock Exchange transactions and was answered, 'It is very important for the Secretary to keep in touch with up-to-date economic questions.'

One of the most delightful people I met in America was Mrs Whitney Straight. She is the only very rich woman I have ever known who was truly generous, which of course is something quite different from being extravagant. She had inherited a large fortune on the death of her husband. He must have been a man of great culture and nobility of character, and had given much of his immense wealth to worthy causes. She carried on his good work and financed some of the most advanced political and literary magazines, helped to put on plays by promising young authors, and assisted other cultural endeavours, whose maintenance would not have been possible without her unobtrusive generosity and her enthusiastic and constructive personality. Later she came to England and was the founder of Dartington Hall School in Totnes.

In Washington I also met Lewis, the president of the American Miners' Federation; a man with a beautiful head and massive, striking features, with flowing black hair and a loose, black cravat: a superb model for a great sculptor. He spoke to me at length and with great passion about conditions in the American coalfields; of the terrific power wielded by the owners in certain bad districts, who used armed forces to break strikes, and held down the workers under a system of near peonage.

I also came across Kenneth Lindsay, who had been a close friend at Oxford, and was later M.P. for Oxford University. I greatly enjoyed seeing him again and exchanging views far from home. He has always retained a boyish enthusiasm for bettering the world, which age and personal difficulties have not dampened.

But perhaps the most extraordinary person I met in the States was Henry Ford. He was credited with being one of the richest men in the world. He also had the reputation for having original and liberal ideas upon political and labour questions. It was partly for the latter reason that Thomas wanted to meet him, to interest him in the work of the International Labour Organisation, and perhaps even in a scheme of his own for establishing an international labour university. Thomas always had at the back of his mind the importance of creating such a centre, where civil servants, students of economics and trade-unionists would come from all over the world and learn what they could from the experience of other countries. A university of this kind would be of great moral support to the International Labour Organisation, which would supply the greater part of the material for research, and might be the source of a far-reaching and enlightened influence.

Ford received us in rather more simple surroundings than we expected. We were ushered straight into his room, which was similar to other rooms on a ground-floor concrete row of offices, some distance from the factories. The upper half of his room was of glass, as in an ordinary factory office, and he was constantly in view of other people in the adjoining rooms. His installation was as modest as that of a manager of any small engineering company.

He was a tall, thin, handsome, ascetic-looking man, clean-shaven, with flowing white hair. He seemed over seventy, though he was still under sixty. When he began to talk he became quite fanatical; and it was quickly obvious that his mania of the moment was anti-semitism. The last war was caused by the Jews. The present unfortunate situation of the world was due to Jewish speculation. Poincaré and Millerand were of Jewish origin and under Jewish influence:

hence the unreasonableness of the French. The Jews were the source of all evil in the world; to search for any other was to be blind to realities. He compared the Jews to fleas and the Gentile to the dog. But the fleas have their purpose; to prevent the dog from going to sleep.

All this came out in a kind of rambling monologue. He attempted to talk about general political questions, but his ideas had no logical sequence. So much so, that it was difficult to carry on any sustained conversation with him. He did not know which currency was the lowest: the dollar, the pound sterling, the Austrian crown, or the mark. He thought Czechoslovakia had an outlet on the Adriatic. He was quite unable to comprehend the views that Thomas and Phelan put forward, and was reduced to spouting out unconnected phrases here and there and repeating his fulminations about the Jews.

He merely had fixed prejudices: anti-semitism, a contempt for France and 'aliens' in general, and a hostility to anyone not engaged in the production of machinery.

Thomas was infuriated by his anti-semitism. His own deep political convictions surged to the surface and brushed aside the original purpose of his visit to Henry Ford. He said that anti-semitism was the argument used by all reactionaries against the influence of liberal ideas. It was the weapon of intolerance employed by the reactionary press in all countries to defile men who had perhaps a greater idealism than many others. He instanced the murder of the German Prime Minister Rathenau, and the splendid record of French Jewish soldiers during the war. Something deep in Thomas was really roused, and I felt it was the best part of his nature.

We met several of Henry Ford's *aides* who ran his propaganda. I imagine he was exploited by such people since, apart from his wonderful engineering activities, he displayed a naïveté and ignorance of world affairs which would have been surprising even in an average schoolboy. I noted he had great difficulty in signing his name. He did so with the painful application of a pupil writing in a copy-book.

While Thomas was trying to explain the difficulties in the way of European reconstruction, Ford uttered such generalisations as 'only one per cent of human energy is required for the ordinary needs of man, the remainder is just a field of experience'. A reporter might have found this profound, and he must often have repeated the phrase before. But he was unable to explain or discuss it. He seemed very pleased with himself after making this kind of remark and looked round the room to see if we were gaping with admiration. I quite expected to see a shorthand-writer scribbling down his words, as did the disciples of Cicero and Socrates, that such thoughts might be preserved for posterity. I soon realised he was a complete megalomaniac.

However, I felt that Ford had a real instinct for publicity. His sayings were of a kind which, if written up and well-prepared beforehand (not resulting from conversation), might make good 'copy' for reporters. His advertising men evidently prepared the right kind of 'dope' and knew the standard that readers of news about murders and baseball would swallow. The best publicity for Ford cars was engineered by putting out innumerable stories showing what bad cars the Fords were. They fell to pieces. They were made of tin. They were available in every colour, so long as the colour was black, etc. These stories prepared by Ford advertising people and disseminated at first through thousands of Ford agents, caught fire on their own, and everywhere popularised the name of Ford. At the time his publicity agents were organising a similar 'spontaneous' 'Ford for President' movement.

When the two-hour discussion was over, Ford asked us to lunch. He seemed to be aware that he had not created the kind of impression he had expected, and therefore confined himself to talking about problems affecting Ford cars and machinery. Here he was in his element and was a different man.

He spent several hours taking us round his wonderful factory, and finally showed us his technical school for teaching the children of his workers. It had to be called a school, Ford said, because of child legislation. Five hundred boys at this school, as part of their instruction, were taught to make spare parts, and the spare parts manufactured in this way more than compensated for the cost of running the school!

Back in Geneva once more, I began to feel that I would like to continue my university education, which had been confined to the two-year shortened course at Oxford, by studying for a Ph.D. This was made easier by the fact that a good deal of my time was spent in London. I therefore became a post-graduate student at the London School of Economics, the newly-formed extension of London University.

At the suggestion of Professor Harold Laski, who was my director of studies, I began to work at a thesis on the Problems of an International Civil Service. The thesis dealt with two main questions. Firstly, how to organise an international conference, provide adequate research and simultaneously obtain the reaction of the various countries in advance, so as to achieve practical results within a short period of time. Secondly, to investigate the best technique for organising an international civil service of multiple nationalities. These were new problems at the time and Professor Laski was very keen that I should do original research, based on the experience of the League of Nations.

Laski was an inspiring and erudite teacher, and a brilliant lecturer; and I greatly enjoyed working under his guidance. It was unfortunate that he tried to mingle his work as a Professor with being the *éminence grise* of the Labour Party. He was brilliantly clever, had a prodigious memory and natural eloquence, but a certain imbalance of character, and personal vanity, made him most unsuitable for any political role. He was always telling us that Ramsay Mac-Donald or other Labour ministers depended entirely on his advice. He had an inferiority complex, which he compensated by inventing all kinds of stories to maintain the myth of his paramount political influence during the period of the Labour Party's first government. But he had neither the strength of character nor the wisdom required for political leadership or sound advice, so his influence eventually fizzled out.

The London School of Economics was a centre of interesting new ideas, and I became closely acquainted with Sir William Beveridge,[1] the Director, and other lecturers like Hugh Dalton.[2] I finally got my Ph.D., and afterwards gave occasional courses of lectures at London University on international affairs.

The young men who joined the League of Nations in its formative period were full of enthusiasm. They believed that it would establish a lasting reign of peace and justice on earth. They were soon disillusioned, when it was seen that the Great Powers, as with the United Nations today, merely used this new organisation as a platform to pursue the same kind of policies that had led to the war.

I shared this disappointment and felt that staying on with the Secretariat would mean that I would gradually be bogged down as a member of an international civil service, whose functions would diminish in importance. So I left the I.L.O. after three instructive years.

[1] Later Lord Beveridge.   [2] Later Lord Dalton.

WORKING MEN'S COLLEGE LIBRARY

Chapter Four

★

FIRST EXPERIMENTS IN BUSINESS

THINKING over what career to adopt, I now decided to study international banking, which would give me a practical insight into some of the other aspects of the problems that had so interested me in Geneva.

Through Mr Alfred Wagg (founder of the banking firm of Helbert Wagg), who was an old friend of Lord Herbert Scott, I met Mr Spencer-Smith, Vice-Chairman of the Bank of England, who suggested that I might go to Vienna as a *volontaire* with the Anglo-Austrian Bank. The Bank of England had just taken over this bank as a constructive step towards consolidating the financial position of Austria.

The other *volontaires* included Francis Glyn (now Sir Francis Glyn, chairman of Glyn, Mills and Company), and Mr Eric Meredith (later managing-director of the Philip Hill banking group). The idea was that young Englishmen of good background would prove an effective counter-weight to the supposedly much too astute Central Europeans who ran the bank. I was put under the guidance of young Fraenkel,[1] of Austrian origin, a nephew of Sir Henry Strakosh. He had just been appointed to the Foreign Exchange Department.

Vienna was a fascinating city at the time. Though most of the population was penniless, the opera was always crowded, and the love of culture and music maintained itself despite political and economic disintegration.

[1] Who later became the very successful managing-director of the Union Corporation.

I followed closely the various measures being taken to stabilise the Austrian currency. Through my former League of Nations connections, I made friends with Cardinal Seipl, the Prime Minister, and Mr Gruenberger, the Foreign Minister, who was most hospitable and kindly introduced me to a wide circle of his friends. Seipl lived in a convent, in two small rooms, and was looked after by the nuns. He was a man of noble character, the only person able to hold together the reins of government of an Austria centred on Vienna, the capital of an empire, but reduced to a fraction of its former size.

The Anglo-Austrian Bank proved a bold but unfortunate venture of Sir Montagu Norman; I found myself completely unsuited to its activities. Owing to the disruption caused by the war, the bank hardly functioned any more as a normal bank. Its industrial credits were being given under interested local advice, and an attempt to control these from London had proved ineffectual. The only profitable side of the business was in currency transactions. Fraenkel was a born dealer, able to manipulate several curved slide-rules at a time, and make profits by playing one fluctuating European currency against another. But this was only a small part of the business. In an attempt to compensate the worsening position, the local managers of the bank indulged in stock-market speculations of the crudest kind.

On my first visit to England I voiced my apprehensions to Spencer-Smith, a most charming and delightful person, steeped in the high traditions of British banking. Because of my lack of practical experience I failed to convince him and it seemed really presumptious for a mere *volontaire* to express general opinions after such a short period. So I left the Anglo-Austrian Bank. A little later this bank, and other large Austrian banks like the Credit Anstalt, failed in a mad speculative crash; and the Bank of England lost the whole value of its investment.

I was twenty-seven. What was I to do now? I was full of

ideas. I thought I might find a useful field of activity in the cinema, which was just then emerging as a successful industry. I had long discussions about it with my uncle Sydney, who greatly encouraged me. I then spent a year studying cinema production in England, in France, in Germany with U.F.A., and finally in the United States.

Through Walter Wanger, who was now production manager of the Famous Players Lasky Corporation, and through Otto Kahn, head of Kuhn Loeb, who had large interests in the cinema industry, I got a warm welcome in American cinema circles in New York and Hollywood.

I spent my first evening in Hollywood with my old friend Robert Nichols, the poet, and his charming bride. They greeted me effusively, for they had been feeling terribly cut off from all their friends. Bitten by the film fever, Nichols had arrived in Hollywood and written to various film people explaining who he was, that he wished to write scenarios, and giving his qualifications. They naturally took no notice, as they were not interested in finding talent. Unused to the American cinema mentality, his arriving unannounced was quite the wrong tactic; as agents and producers were too ignorant of literary reputations in Europe to believe him when he explained his status in England as a writer and poet, instead of having it boosted by publicity agents as was the local custom. Had he been written up beforehand as a distinguished foreign visitor, with introductions from Bernard Shaw or Barrie, all would have been well. The big producing companies would have rushed to get a contract out of him to prevent his being taken up by somebody else. As it was, he was working as one of a number of 'gag' men on Douglas Fairbanks' productions.

I soon told Fairbanks that the Nichols whom he had vaguely noticed on the set was the same Nichols whose brilliant articles in *The Times* on the American cinema industry everyone in Hollywood had been reading and talking

E

about. He was immediately brought into Doug's intimate circle, and his pay and status on the set were raised.

Fairbanks, as in *The Three Musketeers* and *The Thief of Baghdad*, always took the part of some legendary and heroic figure. But he himself was the actual myth he created in his pictures. He was the finest type of virile physical manhood I have ever seen. He was open, generous, hearty and intuitive in his reactions. He was finishing a film called *The Black Pirate* and lived entirely in the atmosphere of the bold, brave, chivalrous Black Pirate. It was fascinating to watch him on the sands, practising a sword and dagger duel with his fencing master. For his subsequent film *Don Q of Zorro* he learned to flick a cigarette out of a man's mouth with a whip with a seven-foot thong. I had so much confidence in his ability that I let him practise on me. These were not mere camera stunts, but an expression of his own skill and zest for life.

Though forty-two, he kept in splendid physical trim, going for an hour's training every evening after work. I joined him in this. He made me run a mile with him, putt-the-weight, and play a new kind of game in a racquet-court with badminton shuttlecocks and tennis-racquet. He was a sportsman to his finger-tips, and had the enthusiasm of a college boy.

His wife, Mary Pickford, was a little woman of great charm, and with an enquiring interest in everything, such as intelligent children have at an impressionable age in their lives. She had a bright perky personality that would have attracted attention anywhere. I first met her in the studio dressed as a ragamuffin. At thirty-two, she was playing the part of a girl of fifteen, and looked it. The film she was acting in was a fairy story about children and giants. She told me she had never had a normal childhood, having been brought up from the age of five as a pantomime girl in a circus. Her longing to take juvenile parts was probably due to a deep-seated need to re-live a life she had missed;

perhaps it was also a compensation for the children who were denied her.

Doug and Mary lived in a kind of fairyland of their own creation. Drawn into the circle, one began to feel that the outside world was of no consequence or interest. But I always felt that Mary Pickford's life was somehow unfulfilled. She had not been able to bridge the gulf that separated her life as a human being and her personality in fairyland.

I found her fascinating, not as a woman but as a delightful child, and I would stay and talk to her for hours. She had so much courage and girlish charm that a man would instinctively feel he wanted to help and protect her. And that was probably her main attraction for Doug, whose nature was so different.

I was told she was a very good business-woman, anxious to exploit her success and make as much money as possible 'whilst the going was good'. She was always urging petty economies on Doug, who would answer, 'What's the good of money unless you spend it.' She told me Doug wanted to leave pictures for six months and travel round the world, saying, 'We'll be old one day, why not enjoy life while we can', which didn't fit in at all with her cautious business instinct.

After a survey of the film industry in Hollywood and Europe, I evolved a scheme to set up a National Film Studio in Brighton, which would give the British film industry the technical facilities it needed to compete with American films. I persuaded the Americans to give their co-operation since they did not wish to antagonise British sentiment, for although the cost of making American films was covered by their exhibition in the U.S.A., their profit was derived solely from their showing in England. I had also secured the help of the Brighton Corporation, who offered the ground for a nominal rent, and had obtained the sympathetic approval of the President of the Board of Trade, Sir Philip Cunliffe-Lister (now Lord Swinton). But at that time I had not the experience, which I was to acquire later, of being able to fashion a good business idea into a form which made it a practical commercial proposition, and to raise the finance required; the amount involved was £200,000. The scheme failed. It had cost me a substantial sum, and all I had gained was further experience. Others were later to take up the idea and establish cinema studios here with first-class technical facilities. But the Brighton offer was never repeated.

I remember showing Sydney what I thought was a well-expressed letter to Otto Kahn on my project. He gave me a piece of advice which I have followed ever since. 'Never try to conduct business negotiations by correspondence, but only in person. Letters are merely of use to confirm something that has already been agreed.'

Faced with the problem in what new direction to divert my energies, I was reminded of a remark by Albert Thomas: 'The life of a politician is generally spent in tackling one immediate problem after another, without having a proper opportunity to think out long-term constructive policies. To be creative, one must at times give oneself an opportunity to lie fallow, so that one's past experience can bear fruit.'

This was really my case. Since the war I had crammed in so much. After a degree, a running blue, the Secretariat of the League of Nations, a Ph.D., a period in Vienna and even doing the Bar exam in my spare time, had come this film experiment. Always meeting new interesting people, and being in contact with new ideas, I had taken in more than I could usefully digest.

I discussed this with Sydney and explained my problem, which met with his ever-sympathetic understanding. At his suggestion I decided to work in a bank for a year. Instead of studying banking from the top floor, as I had done in Vienna, I would do so from the lowest rung of the ladder as a bank clerk. I joined the London branch of the Equitable Trust Company of New York (now the Chase National Bank). It turned out to be one of the most useful and constructive things I had ever done. Of course, I found it very difficult to add up ledgers, but I said to myself, if others could do it without my educational advantages, surely with a little will-power I could also.

The Equitable Trust, under the able management of John Wallace (who only recently retired), did every kind of banking business. It was not too large for me, in doing the accounts, to get to understand the technique of all aspects of its banking activities. Henceforth, as a result of this experience I came to understand banking and business problems in a practical way instead of in part through the eyes of a theoretical economist. After one year I left the bank, having completed my apprenticeship.

In the meantime a situation was developing which appeared catastrophic at the time, but which actually turned out to be the best thing that ever happened to me. I had gradually been running through the capital my father had left, and there only remained a few thousand pounds and the small regular income I had inherited from my mother's trust. This was all due to my not selling out certain of Father's French investments, to my leaving my other investments to the discretion of a broker friend whose speculative advice proved disastrous, and to my having spent my capital too freely. Henceforth I would have to stand on my own feet.

I made up my mind to give up any political ambitions I might have and begin earning my living in earnest.

I decided to go to America and try my luck there. I thought the United States offered greater scope than England for a young man of drive and ambition. And I also felt that if I was going to make a new start on my own it was important for me to be away for a while from the loving, but sometimes overpowering, personalities of Violet and Sydney, who had been like parents to me since Mother's death. If I was to make more mistakes, let me make them on my own, far from the somewhat critical eyes of those I loved.

Chapter Five

★

VIOLET AND SYDNEY

THE greatest influences in my life and the very centre of it were my aunt and uncle, Violet and Sydney. They had no children. They were more to me than parents. They were my most intimate friends for the rest of their lives.

Professor Jack Isaacs, in a talk on the Third Programme in 1949, said of his friend Sydney Schiff, a well-known novelist who wrote under the pen-name of Stephen Hudson:

'Sydney Schiff was born of mixed Jewish and non-Jewish parentage, his father a wealthy banker of Austrian origin, his mother English. For his biography it must be divined between the lines of *A True Story*. Everything is true, except the external details. The persons, the relationships, the agonies, are all true. His family considered him a failure, and not until his second marriage did happiness settle down on him. After the marriage came a new life. The suppressed love of literature and art was released, and it was a new and exciting world to wake into. He bought the work, or helped the struggles, of the most interesting artists of the day, and artists are difficult people to help. He knew Epstein at the time of the Oscar Wilde Memorial, knew Gaudier-Brzeska in his studio under the railway arches, the young Gertler, Bomberg, William Roberts, Currie and Isaac Rosenberg. In their house Marinetti thundered his Futurist doctrines and Caruso parodied him. The walls were hung with pictures by Wyndham Lewis, Picasso, Chirico and John Nash, Roberts,

Gertler, Van Gogh and Matisse. There were friendships, warm friendships, with Katherine Mansfield and with Delius. Hudson was a firm admirer of T. S. Eliot's poetry and a fierce propagandist for 'Prufrock', and together with his old friend, Frank Rutter, he was concerned in the editing of the periodical *Art and Letters* in which appeared the new names of Aldous Huxley, Richard Aldington, Herbert Read, Wyndham Lewis, Ezra Pound, Dorothy Richardson, Katherine Mansfield, T. S. Eliot, Wilfred Owen and the Sitwells, of Modigliani, Wadsworth and Guevara, and in which Hudson himself wrote one of the earliest accounts of Marcel Proust.

'Stephen Hudson was one of the few English friends of Marcel Proust. It came about in a strange way. In 1916 he came across a copy of *Du Côté de Chez Swann*. Nobody in England knew about it or had spoken of it. It entranced him, he marked passages, found, not a kindred soul, he dare not say that yet, but a hero, and before the war had ended had written to him. He tried to find out something about Proust, was told he was just a society clown whose work was unimportant, but wrote nevertheless. Before he met him, he dedicated *Richard Kurt* to M.P., initials which puzzled everybody. And only recently did I learn that M.P. was Marcel Proust. Gradually their friendship grew in intimacy, affection and understanding.

'As with Proust, so it was with Katherine Mansfield. People found themselves telling Hudson things; confidences, and inner truths and revelations. So high a plane of sincerity and truth as he exacted, and so high a level of seriousness, by no means without a sense of fun, demanded self-stocktaking.

'Fascinating as the man Sydney Schiff was, he existed for his friends, some of them at least, as a kind of veil between them and the other half of the double personality — Stephen Hudson, and it is Hudson who will go down to posterity as the creator of *A True Story*. There was a contrast between the fastidious, punctilious, exquisitely courteous and faultlessly dressed military-looking figure — one of the best dressed men in Europe, and the sensitive intelligence from whose agonies sprang novels.'

In 1941 Sydney himself wrote of Violet, 'There is not, and never can be, anyone like her; and she cannot be, even as she never needs to be, anything but herself. Virtue just flows from her very nature as from the everlasting springs. I tell her she deserves no credit for what she is and does for others; the current appraisements, when applied to her, have no meaning. The more deeply one penetrates into her being, the more one realises that the profounder depths are unplumbed and will remain so. In all these more than thirty years we have been married, she has never uttered one word, never made one gesture inconsonant with that nobility of soul which is hers. It is beyond me to express in words what she is to me and in herself.'

Theirs was a most perfect union, and an example of creative love. The depth of their love overflowed to all those they cared for or who appealed to their interest or sympathy, and to me was an inspiration that not only coloured all my life, but formed the ideal I was always seeking, always to be disappointed.

Violet helped to revise all Sydney's work, and was his most constructive critic. He once said to me that if it were not for her divine companionship, his literary output might have been much larger, but that in their interminable conversations together, many long novels had been dissipated.

He had an impulsive, generous and enthusiastic nature, which carried others along with him. Violet shared his many interests, though she had a calmer, more serene disposition. She combined the strong character of a man with the warm charm and sympathies of a woman. She had a capacity for putting others at their ease, listening patiently to what they had to say, and thus drawing them out and making friends with very simple as well as clever people. She was perhaps

Violet and Sydney

interested most of all in young people and their problems.

I have never met anyone with such tact and understanding. Through a chance meeting I had made friends with Alfred Cortot, the pianist, and one of the greatest interpreters of Chopin. I noticed that Violet, when we all spent an evening together, never once mentioned the subject of music, though she was intensely musical and knew most of the great musicians of her time. She afterwards explained to me that for a conversation on music to be interesting *to him*, one would have to be on the same musical level as himself, so she was careful to keep the conversation on the many other subjects which would appeal to him.

After the intellectual isolation of the war, contact with Violet and Sydney and their circle was most stimulating and sometimes even bewildering. Sydney was subject to great ups and downs in his enthusiasms. One day he would discover a house in the country which was just what he wanted. He would buy it at once, explain that living there would be an economy, then spend an enormous amount rebuilding it and making a beautiful garden. He would as suddenly resell it. He did this with his lovely villa at Roquebrune, near Monte Carlo, and again with his beautiful flat in Porchester Terrace, disposing at short notice of all its contents and his collection of modern pictures, and deciding instead to live at Claridge's, so as not to be worried by servant problems, though still keeping Violet's maid, his valet, and a chauffeur. Violet accepted all these sudden changes with complete equanimity. She fell in with his every mood and herself had no feeling for possessions.

These changes were generally due to his wanting to escape from social contacts for a while, and to be free to continue his writing.

For this reason he greatly sympathised with Marcel Proust's attempts to isolate himself from the world.

Knowing him so well, these sudden changes of residence never surprised me, and reflecting on them today I think how wise it is to put personal freedom above the stranglehold of personal possessions. So many of my friends make immense sacrifices to maintain a standard of life they can no longer afford, or retain possessions which, if sold, would enable them to live in the way they would really like.

Sydney had a great sense of humour and dealt in a most original way with members of his family who were always trying to sponge on him. I remember his once telling me, with roars of laughter, that faced with my uncle Charlie's urgent request for a further loan, he replied, 'I'm sorry I cannot afford it, I've just bought a new Rolls-Royce.'

In the same way as he changed houses, he would be most enthusiastic about people, and as suddenly drop them when, as a result of many meetings and endless talks with Violet afterwards, he would have explored to the full the personality that first attracted his interest. Of course, Sydney made a large number of life-long friends like Katherine Mansfield, Marcel Proust and T. S. Eliot, but there was something so kind and warm-hearted in his nature that he often exaggerated the qualities of someone he met for the first time and became no longer interested when he knew them really well. This happened with Aldous Huxley, Ben Nicholson, Osbert Sitwell and W. H. N. Sullivan, and probably with many more names I cannot remember.

Contact with Sydney when I was very young had a disturbing influence. It made me reject many old friendships and social values, without replacing them with others. Sydney had the very highest standards, and anything or anybody that did not come up to them did not count for him. I sometimes adopted his point of view without realising that it was not suited to me and did not spring from the same impulses that inspired him. This often involved me when I was younger in inner conflicts, which, however, gradually resolved themselves as I was able to make my own way in life. But, of course, close contact with him greatly increased the range of my interests. I immensely enjoyed going round with him to various picture galleries and listening to his comments. He used to explain what were, in his opinion, the technical and artistic merits and faults of each picture compared with other pictures by the same artist, or with the work of other painters. He was quick to discover original qualities, or to discern what was imitative of others. When going round a large public gallery, he made a point of concentrating his attention on just a few selected pictures.

Sharing Violet's and Sydney's literary enthusiasms was always exciting, and I read the books that most interested them at the time. My enjoyment of the novels of Henry James had, I believe, been a preparation for Proust, whose books I read and re-read one by one as they came out. And for the first time I began to realise that if one feels an affinity with the sensibility of an author, reading a book may be a real experience in one's own life — like a love affair or a happy or tragic event that enlivens or casts its shadow over one's existence. I only met Marcel Proust once, in 1922, when Sydney gave a party at the Majestic Hotel in Paris for the Diaghilev Ballet. But every meeting, every conversation they had together, was recounted to me in the greatest detail. I think Proust had a special feeling for Sydney, and received support and understanding from him that he got from no one else. Former friends of Proust knew him in a period when he was considered an elegant dilettante, but not a serious writer. Sydney, like him, only started writing seriously when he was over forty. Sydney understood the sensibility of a man of genius whose creative ability had also been heightened by his maturity. Proust had so much to say. Time was running out, afflicted as he was with asthma and other infirmities. In Violet and Sydney he found just that stimulus and understanding which was helpful to him; whilst his older friends belonged to a past that was dead.

At the time, I was shown every exchange of correspondence between Proust and Violet and Sydney, so that the development of their friendship became very much a part of my own life.

In 1919 Sydney had invited Proust to come and stay with them in the country, where he could work in peace and quiet. Proust answered 'If I had not been so ill last week, I would have written to you immediately to let you know how touched I was by your letter. It moved me, it enchanted me, there is a sense of feeling and tact in each phrase. Unfortunately, I am un-invitable. What I mean is that my life is difficult enough when I am isolated, but it would be impossible if my room were cloistered in a household where the activity of others would make me suffer during my bouts of illness and where I would suffer still more by paralysing it. . . . Your offer has moved me all the more because you don't know me. . . . You are for me like a friend of which Sully-Prudhomme has said:

> Let us make no vow to meet,
> The reality of friendship is to feel together,
> The rest is fragile, spare us the farewell.

Writing to Violet in reply to her letter about *Du Côté de Chez Swann* he said, 'Before saying goodbye I want to answer a point of yours which has greatly moved me; "I feel that I will have unhappy moments". I think by this you mean that, too warm-heartedly considering Swann as a living person, you were disappointed to find him becoming less sympathetic and even ridiculous. I assure you, it made me very unhappy to make him like this.

'But I am not free to go against the truth and conceal the law of characters, *Amicus Swann, sed magis amica Veritas*. The nicest people sometimes go through odious periods. I promise that in the next volume, when he defends Dreyfus, he begins to become more sympathetic. Unfortunately, and it greatly pains me, he dies in the fourth volume, and he is not the principal character. I would have loved it if he had been. But art is a perpetual sacrifice of sentiment to truth.'

He again refers to Swann in a copy of *À L'Ombre des Jeunes Filles en Fleurs* which he sent to Violet and Sydney in 1919: 'With the pledge that Swann will once more become sympathetic in subsequent volumes. In heartfelt appreciation of the sympathy from afar, so marvellously understanding, of my two invisible and protective guardian angels from the near and mysterious Island.'

In another letter to Violet he wrote: 'After moving house and a further worsening of my illness, I am, at least provisionally, installed here. My consolation in my new abode, the olive branch that seems to herald better days, comes to me from across the sea, in the form of two revealing writings: an essay on myself in *Arts and Letters* and an admirable novel.[1] I am too weak to talk to you about all these things. And I read English with difficulty. But already a mystery begins to be solved. I can at least bind together what was for me *disjecta membra poetae*: your letters, the essay and the novel are written by the same person (deserving more than Swann all that the essay has to say about books which are a precious study of life's experiences). . . .

'This discovery has enabled me to understand what I had obscurely foreshadowed: I mean that from Mr Schiff's first letter, in the way he spoke of you and your loving influence on him, I had a first premonition. Your letters confirm my assumption and hope: that this pair of readers, as they modestly called themselves, were a married couple who were artists and creators. One does not write certain things in a letter without thereby giving proof that one is capable of the highest achievements. Your profound study of Swann and your novel, which at present is enchanting me, suddenly gave me the clue to the vivid impressions I had received. . . . At last I know you, and it gives me great happiness. Please tell this to Mr Schiff, whose life and spirit I now understand.'

In answer to a long letter from Sydney he wrote: 'I am

---

[1] *Arts and Letters* was edited by Sydney. The novel was *Richard Kurt* by Stephen Hudson, which Sydney dedicated to Proust.

much nearer to Mrs Schiff (I adore the loving tenderness when you mention her) in my choice of acquaintances. I mean that I do my intellectual work in my own mind, and once I am with others I am indifferent to whether they are intelligent, as long as they are kind-hearted and sincere. . . .' And again, 'I do want to know when next you are coming to Paris, for the incredible thing is that I, who never miss anyone, am always longing to be with you.'

A letter that moved me very much was when he wrote to Sydney: 'Part of your letter threw me into a state of deep despair. It was the wonderful phrase on friendship, which ought not to be realised materially (the phrase which ends with these heart-rending words, worthy of the greatest, "so as not to have to endure the end"). You cannot imagine how unhappy this phrase made me. You can readily understand that not seeing even my family for years, not being able to read or write, or eat, or even to get up, with just an occasional outing like the one I made one day to see you, I can only persevere with this awful existence because of the illusion, each day defeated, each day renewed, that this will change. For fifteen years I have been living in hopes rekindled from day to day. And your letter has made me face, in a few moments of bewildering sadness, the reality I do not wish to see. Do not regret it, truth is always beneficial; and then I quickly recovered my courage and returned to my work so as not to think about it. Please keep this confidence for yourself alone (I mean for you and Violet, whom I cannot separate). For I never talk of myself. And when once by chance I meet a human being, I say that the only reason I don't see anybody is because of my work. It would displease me that anyone should think otherwise.'

When Proust died, Sydney wrote a short story called *Céleste*, describing how Proust had managed to finish correcting his final volume, before closing his eyes for the last time. Sydney had always told me that Proust's family never fully appreciated his genius when he was alive. But after his death they published all his immense correspondence, including some intimate letters most unsuitable for publication. This was no doubt the reason why the copies of all Sydney's letters were destroyed after his death, including, I am sorry to say, the wonderful ones he wrote to Proust, who thought so highly of them that he once wrote to Sydney that he ought to ask for 'their return to have them published. . . . For instance, your last letter, the mother-in-law, the concerts, the marvellous old servants, the tree, Henry James: all this is more remarkable than one usually reads in books; and your previous letter about misanthropy, and about the touching relationship between you and Mrs Schiff. It has happened in the history of literature that people have expressed themselves better in correspondence with some particular person, than in fiction or criticism.'

On another occasion, Proust sent Sydney one of his books inscribing in it, 'But what is all this beside your admirable letters . . . which should be counted amongst the writings of lasting worth. Mrs Schiff and you imbue even the most simple things with your own atmosphere, and render them delightful. A banality from you seems to me impossible. Please convey my deep respects to Mrs Schiff *et croyez que je vous aime infiniment*.' Sydney later wrote: 'In re-reading his letters, I realised what a wonderful thing our friendship was, though it came so late in his life. The depth of his feeling is extraordinary and confirms and justifies my inner feeling that Marcel was the man whom of all others in my life I have most loved.'

Violet taught me to sing. For hours and hours, for years and years, she sat patiently at the piano teaching me songs and how to vocalise. To overcome a tendency to sing out of tune I used to practise with tuning forks, which give a small clear sound to copy. Working with a metronome helped my difficulties of rhythm and time. She had a wonderful and inspiring gift as a teacher. Having accompanied such singers as Caruso, and being herself a pupil of Tosti and other famous composers, her interpretation of a song was perfection. I remember her saying: 'It is worth-while working for weeks and weeks to perfect one song. If you can do one song of Fauré with every correct light and shade, you will eventually be able to sing every song of his equally well.' Her teaching me singing was like the gift of a new talent, the bestowal of an enjoyment, a pleasure and relaxation for the rest of my life. One may not always have occasion to express feelings of tenderness and emotion that must lie suppressed. Singing provides an outlet for them, and the quiet practice of a difficult phrase brings with it for me a certain calm and serenity that is a protection from the hardness of the outside world. I have had lessons from many teachers like Elena Gerhardt, Alfred Cortot, Jean de Reszke, Richard Tauber and Pierre Bernac, but they were only to supplement the work I did with Violet.

And, of course, she became my confidante in my love affairs. 'I have just read *Of Human Bondage*,' I once wrote to her. 'It describes much of the torment I have been going through lately. Maugham writes "It is an illusion that youth is happy, an illusion of those who have lost it; but the young know they are wretched, for they are full of the truthless ideals which have been instilled into them, and each time they come into contact with the real, they are bruised and wounded". That is very much what I have felt lately.'

This close and devoted relationship between a son and his mother — for Violet replaced in my heart all the tender feelings I had for my mother — is not without certain handicaps. The ideal mate becomes in the mind a younger version of one's mother. When falling in love, the imagination is apt to attribute these same qualities to the object of that love, only to be bitterly disillusioned with the reality, which can never be an exact copy. Or again, this ideal, though suitable as a sister or a mother, may not be the one most suited to one's nature and personality.

Sydney had a wonderful way of giving me the benefit of

his own thoughts and experiences. He never lectured me on some general principle, but waited until some episode occurred in my own life and then helped me to work out the moral for myself. When on the League of Nations, I once told him that I had met Arthur Henderson on some committees and wondered how such a dull man could have become Secretary of State for Foreign Affairs. Sydney replied that it was not unusual for young people to find fault with men in prominent positions by picking up some obvious weakness, but in the case of Arthur Henderson it would seem more profitable if I studied what were the *qualities* that enabled a man of humble origin to rise to one of the highest offices in the Cabinet. I then discovered, amongst other traits, that Arthur Henderson was an indefatigable worker, was modest, and therefore did not inspire jealousy in others, and was trusted because of his fairness, impartiality and personal integrity.

I owed so much to my beloved Violet and Sydney, who had helped to guide me in my youth and who continued to be the cherished friends with whom I could discuss every subject with complete freedom, and whose interest in the arts, literature and music continued to be such an inspiration in my life. As they grew older, it gave me enormous pleasure if I could do small things to make life easier for them and to feel that they could lean on me more and more for support.

Violet was rather impractical as regards material arrangements, having been brought up in the Victorian era when servants were plentiful and trained housekeepers saw to domestic problems. Sydney had got extremely fussy as he grew older, and worried about the details of packing. Everything he thought they might need, and much more, had to be neatly put into the large number of trunks that it was customary to travel with in those days. He often said he wished he were like me: able to leave on a journey at a moment's notice, throw what I needed into a couple of hand-bags and not worry if any item was forgotten. But his meticulous nature had a

F

happier counterpart in the care with which he worked at his novels. He would spend hours searching for the right phrase to express his thoughts, or in selecting the most suitable design for the decoration or arrangement of his house. He was a perfectionist in everything he touched.

But with his temperament, travelling abroad was a worrying experience for him. A visit to Paris by the Golden Arrow entailed registering luggage in London, a customs examination of the luggage at Dover and Calais, the effort of finding porters on both sides of the Channel as well as at both ends of the journey.

Finding him one evening in a dejected mood over their next morning's departure for Paris, I told Sydney not to give it another thought for I would go with them to Paris and see to all the tiresome details of the journey. I was delighted next day, when he left everything in my hands, that the Channel crossing was smooth, and the journey pleasant and uneventful. I saw everything packed into the private car from the Ritz Hotel that met us on arrival at the Gare du Nord in Paris, and to their surprise said goodbye to them, explaining that an urgent business appointment next morning forced me to return by the next train.

Chapter Six

★

BUSINESS IN THE U.S.A.

DESPITE my previous setbacks, I was in an optimistic mood when I landed in New York in 1925. I called on various banks to offer my services and finally obtained a very interesting job with Blair & Co., who, with Morgans, Kuhn Loeb and Dillon Read, were the leading investment bankers in Wall Street. At the time Blair were floating large European loans; I was lucky enough to be successful in this field, and soon earned a really substantial salary.

Working in the United States is a marvellous experience for a young man. There is no prejudice against youth or new ideas. On the contrary. New ideas are welcomed, as most fortunes have been made trying out something new. There was none of that antagonism that exists in financial circles in England, which generally condemns a pioneer for being 'speculative' or 'dangerous' because he starts a commercial development on novel lines, and only considers him a sound business man when he has reached the sixties. When I was a young man, men like Isaac Wolfson and Simon Marks were spoken of in those terms, because they pioneered the first large-scale development of multiple shops.

In the United States it is traditional to scrap existing machinery and replace it with new, to cut losses and start afresh. The whole atmosphere is one of vigour and new enterprise. I am quite certain that any modest success I may subsequently have achieved in England was due to my early experience over there.

In America I also had a very pleasant social life. I used to sing a good deal at my friends' houses. This was how I first met Charlie Chaplin, at a party at Mrs Vanderbilt's. I had sung a song from the operetta *Mozart* by Renaldo Hahn, which went:

Depuis ton départ, mon amour,
Ta pensée ne me quitte pas.

and Charlie, with his spontaneous enthusiasm, begged me to sing it again, and this was the beginning of our acquaintance.

We did not work at the bank on Saturdays, so nearly every Friday afternoon I took the train to Poughkeepsie, where I hunted with the Milbrook at the invitation of Percy Rockefeller, who was joint-master with Joe Thomas. He mounted me on wonderful horses, sometimes former Grand National runners, and I stayed at his house and enjoyed his weekend parties. He could not have been kinder. The hunting was superb. The jumps were all post and rail, which I much preferred to the kind of jumps in the hunting field at home. Well mounted, one was quite safe and always saw the ground clearly before and after the jump. The hounds were smaller and had a much better cry than English foxhounds. This, Joe Thomas told me, was due to the basic character-istics of British foxhounds being gradually spoiled by the requirements of dog shows.

I once asked Rockefeller how it was that I hardly saw any young men at the meet. He explained that as I was an English-man, it was of course different. But he could not otherwise invite young men unless they were also millionaires, as they would want to sell him real estate, shares or insurance policies, which would be intolerable. It was difficult to make him believe that with the Pytchley Hunt at home one met many influential people, but that it would be considered against the most elementary code of decent manners to make use of someone met in this way, for any business advantage.

I became very friendly with Joe Thomas, who devoted

his time almost entirely to the hunt, and helped him to edit a book he was writing on hounds. In England, as a rich man living in fine style, a splendid rider, and running one of the best packs of hounds in the country, his social status would have been very high. In America a few years before the Wall Street crash, nobody was considered anybody unless he was engaged in the prevalent feverish pursuit of making more money.

Up to that time the Americans had subscribed to large slices of European loans, brought out by European banks. They were now initiating foreign loans themselves. Jean Monnet, with Blair, was responsible for important loans to Italian public utilities like the Montecatini Company. Blair's most ambitious initiative was a $70 million Stabilisation Loan to Poland. A loan to a foreign government for reconstruction purposes entailed the preparation of a plan to ensure that the country's finances were established on a sound basis. An American committee of experts was set up, and a report prepared by Mr Benjamin Anderson, the economist of the Chase Bank. I was later asked my opinion of the report, and thanks to my experience on the League of Nations and in Austria, I spotted a serious flaw in the proposals. The Polish budget was balanced on paper, but not in reality. Short-term borrowings were being used for long-term lending to agricultural mortgage societies, and for the building of roads and railways, thus creating a large deficit in liquid resources. Soon after I had convinced Blair of this position, I became the economic adviser to the committee, which included Mr Foster Dulles of the legal firm of Sullivan and Cromwell, whom I then met for the first time. This is characteristic of go-ahead American methods. They are quite prepared to take a chance and give high responsibility to a young man to an extent unheard of in Britain.

I completed the plan for the reorganisation of Polish finances and the loan was a great success. I also went to San

Francisco and placed a section of the loan with Giannini, the head of the Transamerica Corporation, the largest deposit bank in America.

I was naturally very pleased with myself over this and asked Mr Elisha Walker, the chairman of Blairs, for a substantial bonus. In England it would have been the normal thing to prove my worth before asking for extra remuneration, assuming that it would then be readily accorded. Wall Street standards were different. Elisha Walker said he greatly appreciated my work but that, regarding extra pay, I had 'better charge it up to experience'. I was slowly learning the ways of the world. I was not particularly upset about this, but it was an 'experience' that I did not permit to occur again.

Jesse Lasky, whom I had met before in London and Hollywood, asked me to lunch whilst passing through New York. He was managing-director of the Famous Players Lasky Corporation, the largest cinema producing company in America. He had started life as a saxophone player and, with his friend Adolf Zukor, had got into films in their early stages. Zukor was a man with great financial flair and business ability. Lasky was a genial, pleasant fellow; outwardly he seemed to express the strong decisive confidence of success, but in reality he was not very sure of himself. After discussing the position of his company, I convinced him that I could bring about enormous financial savings in the production side of his business, if I were allowed to make a thorough investigation. I 'sold' him the idea and he begged me to take it on. Discussing the remuneration I would require, I remembered that he thought nothing of tying up artists on options for large sums, and that unless I asked a comparable amount, he would think less of my capability. We settled for $25,000 and my expenses for a three-month period in Hollywood, where I would attend all directors' meetings.

It was July and New York was beginning to be oppressively hot, so the move to the pleasant Hollywood climate was a relief. Blair was most friendly about my going and offered to take me back later. It was not unusual in America even for partners in banking firms to leave at a moment's notice, if they could improve their financial position; and neither sentiment nor friendship were allowed to stand in the way of advancement. In England, directors usually have the support of senior clerks and excutives who have been with the company for years, and who are happy to serve it faithfully for adequate remuneration. Over there, these same people would always be thrusting forward to displace the 'boss'. This situation may give young men a quicker chance of promotion, but it compels top American executives to overwork and overstrain themselves, and often leads to premature death. This is why the greatest wealth in the U.S.A. belongs to the widows!

When I arrived in Hollywood, the executives of the Famous Players said they were ready to answer any question I would like to put to them. I told them I wanted to study the accounts and ask the questions afterwards. So much easy money was being made by film companies that they had not yet caught up with waste and inefficiency. Famous Players produced seventy full-length pictures a year, and were always short of stories. Yet every executive who went to Europe bought plays and stories, but no proper record was kept of these, and I found the company had about $8,000,000 worth of them locked away. In case a 'take' went wrong, it was the custom for a dozen cameras to duplicate each 'shot', and these were all developed. The cost of printing twelve times the amount of film actually used came to enormous sums. The elementary financial recommendations I put forward pleased Lasky, though some of the top executives who benefited indirectly from the existing state of affairs were not so satisfied.

My stay in Hollywood certainly cured me of ever being attracted by an actress. A manager or producer, who could

get them a job or advance their careers, however old or un-
savoury, was more important in their eyes than any virile,
intelligent young man. And becoming a star made most of
them incredibly vain and self-important. Their lives were
artificial, their only talk was about 'pictures' or their 'public',
and for me they had no glamour whatsoever. From a commercial point of view it was necessary to build up personalities, but it was amusing to see greatly publicised world
figures like Pola Negri from the point of view of the company
that employed them. They were considered simply as
commercial chattels, to be taken up or dropped according to
the current box-office trends. When I was there, Famous
Players, hearing that Pola Negri's popularity was waning,
decided to reduce their possible loss by selling the remaining
two years of her contract to an English company at half the
cost of the contract.

Amongst the personalities I met in Hollywood, and whom
I used to meet when later they visited Europe, was Adolphe
Menjou, who started life as a French waiter in Chicago and
graduated upwards to play the part of sophisticated French
aristocrats in films that made him a world celebrity. He had
brought his latest picture-postcard-looking wife to Paris,
and one afternoon we three were having tea with Violet and
Sydney at the Ritz. An elegantly dressed old man, with a
flower in his buttonhole, went past with a large bulldog
pulling at the lead. He bowed gravely to Sydney, who said to
Menjou, 'That is Count Boni de Castellane.' Menjou's face
lit up with excitement as he exclaimed to his wife, 'That is a
real Count!'

Whilst in Hollywood I persuaded Famous Players to make
the first large-scale gangster film. Up till then thrillers were
'quickies' made as cheap stunt films by independent
companies. The story I suggested was by Ben Hecht about
Chicago. I proposed Sternberg as director, and the company
insisted on one of its existing executives, Mr Shulberg, as
producer, to prevent the film from becoming too 'arty'. The

picture was a great success and Sternberg, whom I had originally met under the name of Stern, later promoted himself to Von Sternberg.

I might have obtained an interesting job in Hollywood but, except for Wanger, who was really cultured and had a high standard in his business dealings, I found the leaders of the American film industry unpleasant to work with. Blair wanted me to return to them. But I was anxious to get back to England again.

My stay in America had been a further instructive apprenticeship. Besides, there had been the added interest of lecturing on International Affairs at Columbia University, and also addressing large public meetings of the Non-Partisan Association, which corresponds to our League of Nations Union. I found American audiences much more interesting than British ones, anxious to hear what was going on in the world outside, and eager to respond to noble aspirations.

One evening at Columbia University a very pretty student, whom I had noticed before in the front row gazing up at me with large blue eyes, told me how much she had appreciated hearing me. I felt flattered and asked what particular aspect of my lectures had interested her most. 'I am afraid I did not understand very much about the subjects', she answered. 'But I have so enjoyed listening to your Oxford accent.' Needless to say, I asked her out to dinner.

It was lucky I left America when I did. Had I stayed I am sure I would have been engulfed in the Wall Street crash like so many of my friends. Markets were moving up in a frenzied way, and cautious and honest standards of business seemed to have disappeared. In New York I had discussed the idea with Blair of their starting an Investment Trust, on the lines of those of Robert Fleming in England. They eventually issued 1,000,000 shares of $5 each, and I had supposed they would have started the market at under $6, which should have left a margin for their profit and initiative. The public rushed to buy the shares, each representing a diversified investment worth $5, and the price started at $28 a share and rose to $50. It was just highway robbery, but was in line with the promotions of other American banking firms of high standing. The Blair partnership at the time was supposed to be worth nearly £200 million; a few years later many of the partners were asking me to find them jobs in London. Zukor once told me he had been offered $100 million for his cinema holdings. 'But what shall I do with the money?' He lost everything in the crash, and for the rest of his life lived on a small pension from the company he had created.

Chapter Seven

★

THE CITY (PRE-WAR)

WHEN I returned to London several opportunities presented themselves. Mr F. A. Szarvasy, one of the leading London financiers and a director of Martins Bank, invited me to join the Board of the General Theatre Corporation, a new £3,000,000 cinema-theatre combine he was forming. He also discussed my joining the British, Foreign and Colonial Corporation, at that time the most prominent issuing house in the City.

I also had an approach from another quarter which arose from quite unexpected circumstances, and which formed the basis of my subsequent career in the City. Staying with Violet and Sydney in the hotel at Caux in Switzerland, I met a charming little old man called Mr Brandford, with whom I had talks about certain problems of social reform. He was director of some City companies, but his lifelong interest was the creation of the Sociological Society, a cause to which he gave the larger part of his private fortune. Hearing that I was trying to find a position in the City, he mentioned this to his colleague, Mr Whitcroft of the Law Debenture Corporation. As a result, Mr Whitcroft arranged for me to meet Mr M. S. Myers, who had built up one of the most successful broking and issuing houses in the City. Myers and his partner, Mr Goetz, who were both over sixty, were looking for a young man as a potential partner, as those listed as partners at the time were purely dealers and clerks without any say in the direction of the business. I went to see Mr

Myers at his office at 19 Throgmorton Avenue. After an
hour's talk, he offered me £8,000 for a trial period of one
year, adding that if I was not satisfied I could call it a day
after eight months and receive the full £8,000. If all went
well, at the end of the first year the terms of a partnership
would be considered. Quite apart from the interest of the
job, I was drawn to a man who, meeting me for the first time,
immediately made me such an attractive offer. I was still
under thirty.

Little Mossy Myers, as he was known, was about five foot
three, but big in every other way. He was never petty in his
financial dealings. The firm was making average profits of
over £200,000 a year, so if he could get the right man, a few
thousands here or there did not matter. One of the outstanding businesses that he had recently done was the
financing of the purchase of Allied Newspapers for the Berry
brothers (later Lord Camrose and Lord Kemsley). They
bought Allied Newspapers from the late Sir Edward
Hulton for £6,000,000, and recapitalised the company into
£6,000,000 8-per-cent Preference shares and £2,000,000 in
Ordinary shares. This was financed by Myers making a
public issue of £6,000,000 8-per-cent Preference shares and
giving those who underwrote the issue of Preference shares
10 per cent of the Ordinary shares in Allied Newspapers.
The public who bought the newspapers enormously over-
subscribed the Preference shares, and this resulted in the
Berry brothers owning 90 per cent of the Ordinary shares of
Allied Newspapers in exchange for the *Sunday Times*.

The main profits of the firm of Myers & Company came
through making large issues. The profits from the stock-
broking business largely depended on these issues and on the
private business of large clients such as Sir John Ellerman,
Solly Joel, Lord Dewar, the Berry brothers, Sir John Vestry,
Sir James Dunn and many others.

I soon discovered that the best way I could help Myers
was by relieving him of most of the tedious detail work,

such as the legal and technical side of the firm's immense issuing business; but not at this stage trying to get any new business myself.

When this arrangement had been going for about four months, Felix Goetz asked me to dinner, but did not talk business until after the long sumptuous meal was over. He then started to complain about 'that silly little Mossy', in a Potash and Perlmutter style, saying how stupid he was to have made arrangements to pay me such a large amount. He finally suggested as a compromise that I should reduce the £8,000 guarantee to £5,000, thinking he was doing a very good piece of business for the firm. I told him that if he was dissatisfied with the arrangement I would prefer to cancel it altogether and henceforth receive 50 per cent of all the profits I brought to the firm, without any guarantee.

From then on I went out to obtain new issues and secure as clients many of the large insurance companies and City institutions which the firm had not previously dealt with. One of the first issues I originated was for Richard Fairey.[1] He had gone round the City trying to raise new finance, but nobody would back anything so speculative as the aviation industry. I have always found it better to back a man than a particular industry. Fairey was certainly an example of this. He was six feet four inches tall and the kind of man who exuded self-reliance and quiet efficiency. During the war the government had told him that if he would start a company with a capital of £2,000, they would give him the orders; since then he had never looked back. 10 per cent of the capital had been put up by his solicitor, Mr Charles Crisp. Thanks to Mr Crisp's advice, the company had been put into liquidation every eleven months and had thus escaped all taxation. He now wanted additional capital to introduce his shares on the market. As it happened, New York was just beginning to popularise shares in the aviation industry, and I was able by telephone to get a sufficient

[1] Later Sir Richard Fairey.

American participation to induce the City institutions to
hazard their money in the Fairey Aviation Company, which
developed from strength to strength in future years.

Another issue I originated was for the Ecko Company,
for E. K. Cole, a clever radio inventor living in Southend.
At that time the radio industry was largely seasonal, the
selling season being the winter months; the company, which
was in Southend, recruited its female labour amongst women
working in the tourist industry in the summer. This was the
first City finance for the radio industry.

Goetz's proposal to revise my first year's agreement with
Myers turned out very satisfactory for me, as my first year's
earnings were over £27,000. I then joined the firm as a full
partner, agreeing not to take out more than £5,000 a year
after tax, the balance accruing to build up my capital in the
firm. This balance eventually became the largest capital in
the business. Owing to high taxation, it is no longer possible
today for young partners through their earnings to buy out
senior partners in private partnerships, and this is especially
hard in professions like that of solicitors or accountants,
where the total earnings are subject to supertax without any
allowance for reserves as in industrial companies.

My first year in the City proved that one can make a
success there without having any personal friends in
City circles. People do business with you because it is to
their financial advantage, and friendship does not enter into
it. I had certainly never met any of these people before.
Reacting strongly from my American experience, I also
never did so-called entertaining to attract business. Rich
men are not lured by the offer of a free meal; and the happy
friendships that so often develop as a result of business
contacts grow naturally without the pressure of a so-called
'expense account'.

During my ten years with Myers, the firm underwrote
over £150 million of new industrial issues, many of which
were originated by me. I still found myself connected with

the film industry, as Myers had financed the film interests of the Ostrer Brothers, who owned the Gaumont-British Picture Corporation and the Provincial Cinematograph Company, which had recently absorbed the General Theatre Corporation. I initiated the provision of finance for John Maxwell's Associated British Picture Corporation, for whom we placed £6,500,000 of new securities with the public. What a contrast with a few years previously when, not knowing the technique of raising money, I had been unable to find the finance required for my £200,000 scheme to start a National Film Studio at Brighton!

Isidore Ostrer, the eldest of the three brothers, had a most astute financial brain, and perhaps deserved greater public credit than he ever received for being the pioneer of the British Film Industry and for starting the biggest chain of cinema theatres in England. This was probably because he kept himself very much in the background, and was known to the public more for his financial activities than for the constructive building up of his group. Non-voting A shares had not yet been invented, but Isidore Ostrer's ingenious mind conceived the creation of his £600 company, the Bradford and Municipal Trust, which controlled the Gaumont-British Corporation, and its large subsidiary companies, with assets running into millions of pounds.

In New York and Hollywood I was concerned in the negotiations for the sale of this voting trust to the Fox Film Company of America and later to Associated British Pictures. As much as £1,800,000 was finally offered for this £600 company!

My discussions with Joe Schenk of Fox Films were long drawn out, as he was always consulting his brother Nick Schenk, chairman of Metro-Goldwyn-Mayer, and then changing the basis of the negotiation. One day, being some-what upset by their horse-trading tactics, aggravated by the intense summer heat of New York, I suggested breaking up the meeting for an hour. I took a taxi, went straight to the

Metropolitan Museum and sat quietly admiring one of my favourite pictures, *Summer* by Breughel. This had a most calming effect, and I returned to the fray with the two 'skunks' (the code name in my cables home), refreshed and full of fight. These negotiations dragged on and I had to continue them in Hollywood. But this visit had its lighter moments as I again met Charlie Chaplin.

One afternoon I was playing tennis at Miss Constance Bennett's luxurious home. The foursome included Errol Flynn, Paulette Goddard and myself. I had never met Paulette Goddard before and was delighted when at the end of the afternoon she invited me to go and see Charlie, saying warmly, 'I'm sure he would love to get to know you'. I dined with them that evening and Paulette discreetly left us alone after dinner. We talked until the early hours of the morning.

I felt that though Charlie was very much part of the Hollywood scene, he was curiously detached from it and not influenced by its shoddy values and unreality. He was a free, independent spirit. That evening he was very depressed and seemed relieved to be able to talk to me.

I realised he was deeply in love with Paulette. She had an appealing, gamine type of beauty, and was intelligent and spontaneous. Charlie longed to change and improve her to fit into some ideal of his own imagining. He hated her to drink and had offered her a thousand shares of General Motors if she would stop drinking for even three months. He would have liked to make her a great dramatic actress, but though she appreciated him, his genius as a producer and an artist did not make the emotional appeal he so ardently desired. His continuous efforts to change and improve her merely created resentment. This is what happens in so many marriages.

I saw a lot of Charlie and Paulette during that visit; and ever since, even if we have been separated for years at a time, Charlie and I have always resumed our friendship as easily as if we had met the previous day.

A few years later I had plans with a group of City associates to buy United Artists, and become its chairman. United Artists were a group of independent producers, including Charlie Chaplin, Douglas Fairbanks, Mary Pickford, Walter Wanger and Sam Goldwyn. The producers had shares in the parent company, which helped to provide finance for each individual production and made a profit on the distribution of films. I had agreed the terms in London and all seemed settled when I arrived in Hollywood. But at the last moment Sam Goldwyn insisted on changing the terms so the deal never came off.

There was an amusing sequel to my United Artists negotiations. Two years later the evening papers in London were full of headlines that Alexander Korda had bought United Artists. That night Korda rang me up from New York, at a time when calls cost £20 a minute, to say, 'You've probably read in the papers that I have bought United Artists. I've fixed everything except the money. Can you help?'

Originally I had offered $5,000,000 (at that time £1,000,000) for the business and had arranged to provide a further £1,000,000 of working capital by the public issue of Preference shares. I explained this to Korda on the telephone and he told me the extra million was absolutely necessary as without the additional cash the producing units might 'go bust'. When he told me, however, that the profits which had been £350,000 at the time of my original offer were now halved, I replied that they were too low to justify an issue of the extra £1,000,000 for working capital. His comment was: 'Well, let's not bother about the working capital. Let's buy the business anyhow and hope for the best.' It was like a comic situation in a Marx Brothers film. Korda had little money at the time, his later fortune was made because he was able to acquire options at low prices on old United Artists films. These became very valuable during the war and later for television.

Just after the Wall Street crash I went to the United States

G

and offered to find finance for some of the American industrial giants, by making issues for their very successful British subsidiary companies. At that time Wall Street was licking its wounds after the disastrous slump, and anyone offering cash in New York received a warm welcome.

In these exceptional circumstances I found many millions of pounds for the American Radiator Company (Ideal Boilers & Radiators Ltd), the Monsanto Chemical Company, Kelsey Hayes Wheel, Briggs Motor Bodies, Crown Cork & Seal, and Ruberoid.

The biggest deal I initiated was a proposal to buy the Argentine subsidiary of the Armour Company of America. The amount involved was £14 million, which was to be found by issuing Debentures, Preference and Ordinary shares, on the London market. My negotiations were with Elisha Walker, my former 'boss' in Blair & Company, and now chairman of both Kuhn Loeb and the Armour Company. We discussed the terms of the eventual division of the profits; he suggested 40 per cent, 60 per cent. I said I was agreeable to 60 per cent for us and 40 per cent for our American associates, and reminded him of his telling me to 'put it down to experience' when I left Blair ten years previously! The position was now reversed, as my firm was to underwrite the issue. However, we settled on a fifty-fifty basis, but the deal did not eventualise. The accountants in the Argentine, not uninfluenced by the fat fee involved, insisted on working out a monthly average for the value of the pound sterling over the ten-year period of the profit statement. This delayed the provision of the auditors' certificate by nearly a year, and a change in market conditions made the transaction no longer feasible.

One of the largest companies I was concerned with was Montague Burton Limited. The company was the biggest multiple-tailoring store group in the world, and we had originally made an issue of £2,000,000 7-per-cent Preference shares. The company was always in need of funds, for

Montague Burton was continually putting up new shops, and had no plans for long-term finance. Mr Philip Hill, who was the financial 'take-over' bidder of those days, offered £1,000,000 of mortgage money at ½ per cent below the normal rate. Burton, who was a genius in his line of business but naïve in large-scale finance, let Philip Hill have the latest audited accounts and listened to his suggestions for a financial scheme conceived with the intention of getting control of the company. Philip Hill proposed the formation of a property company which would hold all the freehold and leasehold shops. The property company would issue securities, the interest of which would be covered by a large rental from the parent company. This I thought a dangerous situation as the rental was so high that a modest fall in profits might endanger it. To protect the Preference holders of Montague Burton, I took part in the negotiations with Philip Hill.

One of the critical points was also that Burton's would control the ordinary shares of the property company. Burton was induced by Philip Hill to go on with the scheme and a circular was sent out to the shareholders. I then insisted that Philip Hill should confirm in writing that Burton's would control the property company. Philip Hill said that as a circular had gone out to the shareholders, Burton could do nothing about it, as the banks were anxious to have a large overdraft repaid, and on reconsideration he *insisted* on the control of the property company.

To save the situation I arranged a meeting of the representatives of the Preference shareholders, which included Mr Crump of the Prudential, Mr Walter Whigham of Robert Fleming, and Mr A. H. Wynn of the Mercantile Investment. They agreed to underwrite immediately a public issue of £1,000,000 6½-per-cent Preference shares and £1,000,000 5-per-cent Debentures (part of £3,000,000 issue), the balance of £2,000,000 Debentures to be sold gradually over the year. Next day I acquainted Philip Hill with the position.

He was a great, big, powerful, ruthless-looking man, who had done enormous transactions and was at the peak of his success. To my surprise he had tears in his eyes when his scheme fell through. Seeing him suddenly overcome with emotion, I felt quite sorry for him. The incident did not prevent us doing business again and my getting a £50,000 fee for my firm in connection with the amalgamation of Macleans and Beechams.

I immediately afterwards went on the Board of Montague Burton Ltd as deputy chairman, and prepared a complete programme of reorganisation, both as regards finance and management. So often when a successful company has developed rapidly under its founder, the main problem of the business is to decentralise it so that the ever-growing detail of the organisation can be carried out by responsible executives, leaving the chairman leisure for thinking out general policy and particular problems requiring the benefit of his specialised knowledge and experience. I helped to bring about a long-term planning of the shop development by always getting finance in advance. For this purpose we arranged for the issue of a further £5,000,000 of securities, in addition to the £6,000,000 we had already provided. The company opened up an additional 200 shops in the next four years, a greater rate of development than was ever considered possible in the past.

To facilitate the decentralisation of the company, best attempted when he was away, Burton absented himself from his business for the first time in his life and went for a world tour. Whilst he was away the shop-stewards threatened a strike, despite the fact that the Leeds factory was considered a model of its kind as regards welfare and the wages were above those prevalent in the trade. The trade unions appealed to me to uphold their authority, as against the unreasonable demands of the shop-stewards who were trying to by-pass the normal procedure of negotiation. This is where my former International Labour Office experience came in. I stood by the trade unions and faced a general strike, refusing to negotiate except through the local trade-union leaders. The strike lasted a few weeks, but finally the authority of the trade union was restored, and I understand that as a result there was no important strike in the industry for the next twenty years. The canteen was kept open during the strike for the benefit of the strike pickets, and the company generously paid out benefits for the families who had suffered hardships during the strike. All this eventually brought about much happier labour relations.

This experience gave me a great liking for participating in the actual management of a company, as distinct from just finding money for its development; henceforth my main business interest was to concern myself actively in the management of industrial concerns as well as providing finance.

Another large issue we made was in connection with the amalgamation of Sears and Freeman, Hardy & Willis. This was an amalgamation conceived by Mossy Myers with Sir Nutcombe Hume of the Charterhouse Trust, and involved £3,750,000 of new finance. The company was to be the subject of a take-over bid by Charles Clore twenty years later, on whose behalf I underwrote further finance.

A most pleasant experience was doing business with Lord Camrose and his brother Lord Kemsley. The closeness of their association was unusual. They had a joint banking account. Any shares that were bought for one brother were bought in equal amounts for the other. They continued this arrangement until Lord Kemsley, who had been a widower for many years, eventually remarried. In the brotherly partnership in the newspaper, Lord Camrose largely dealt with the editorial policy and his brother the business side. Camrose never forgot what he had owed to Myers when he first bought the control of Allied Newspapers. He had been approached by numerous banks offering to find new finance for his newspaper developments, but he said as Myers had helped him at the start, he would never consider changing. We made issues of many millions for Allied Newspapers, Kelly's Directories, Iliffe Press, etc. We never signed a contract, our agreement was verbal only, and after one particular issue, which was a difficult one, Lord Camrose gave us an extra £10,000 fee. He was a splendid example of a leader of industry, having started from modest circumstances and reached the top rung of the ladder of success. His courage, initiative and business ability were combined with all the best traits of aristocratic tradition. He never sought to take advantage of anyone in his business dealings and was generous in small and large matters alike.

When my partnership came up for renewal in 1938, it gave me the opportunity of retiring. Though I was contributing more than half the profits, Myers was at times a little jealous that someone half his age should be taking such an important part in directing the policy of his own firm. Feeling certain that the war was coming, I was apprehensive of leaving all my capital in a partnership with unlimited liability, especially as Goetz used much of the firm's capital to finance his unsuccessful speculations. I also wanted to be free to go on the boards of companies and take an active part in their management, which Myers always opposed, wanting me to devote all my time to the firm's business.

I therefore retired from Myers & Company and from the Stock Exchange under a friendly arrangement with my former partners, and set up the Ocean Trust as an issuing house, owned wholly by myself. It had a capital of £100,000, so that my loss on any one transaction would be limited to this sum, and if a war came its activities could be temporarily curtailed, without affecting the employment of a large number of staff as with Stock Exchange firms; and my new directors were on a profit-sharing basis without liability on their part, my principal young director being Lord Long.

I had met him in rather unusual circumstances. One of my best friends was George Lowther, whose father, Colonel

John Lowther, was Master of the Pytchley Hunt. I used to keep three horses at Guilsborough and hunt on occasional Fridays and every Saturday, in what I believe is the biggest jumping country in England. We both enjoyed the excitement of the hunt and spent most weekends together. I used to be invited out to dinner nearly every Friday and Saturday to one of the many hospitable homes in the district, where the men would appear in white ties and scarlet evening dress with hunt buttons. George, wishing to do me special honour, asked me to stay with him one weekend, when he said he would invite his four best girl-friends and his four best men-friends. And that is how I met David, who was the most enjoyable of companions. He wanted to go into the City and, as I hate doing things alone, he joined the Board of the Ocean Trust.

I was specially anxious for new activities that could help me to forget an unhappy love affair. Among the young people included in Violet and Sydney's magic circle was my cousin Renée. She was then twenty-one and was studying piano and singing at the Royal College of Music. I really got to know her well for the first time when I came to the Palace Hotel, Caux, where she was staying with them for a winter holiday. I admired her beauty, her adaptability and her gay and happy disposition. I taught her to ski. We practised duets together, which she accompanied on the piano. We danced a lot in the evenings and were united in our devotion to Violet and Sydney. We were so happy together: it was inevitable that we should fall in love.

Remembering only too vividly the tragedy of my mother's first marriage to her cousin, both Violet and Sydney, and Renée's parents strenuously opposed our marriage, pointing out that we were not only cousins on my father's side, but also more distantly on my mother's. In the end we decided to part. I did not see her again for years, because ours was not the kind of love that could be turned into a so-called 'friendship'. At that time we could have no idea that much later, by a strange miracle, we would be able to marry and 'live happily ever after'.

To escape sombre thoughts, I returned to my favourite Swiss mountains and persuaded my old friend Stanley Spencer to join me there. I thought it might be a source of inspiration for him to see village life in the mountains, where religion plays such a vital and dominant part in the lives of the people.

I had met Stanley years before through my uncle Sydney, who had a marvellous understanding of painting and was very sympathetic towards the modern trend of his time. Sydney had bought his first Stanley Spencer picture when the artist was still a student at the Slade. It was, as so many of his later works, a mystical subject. He also took me to see the murals Spencer had painted for the chapel of the almshouses at Burghclere. These large paintings are little known because they are in so remote a place. They are, I believe, the finest he ever did.

Stanley came to Saas-Fee, the beautiful old village where I was staying 7,000 feet up, just below the glaciers. At that time it could only be reached by a steep, stony track, and in fact mules were the chief means of transport. To see Stanley on muleback was really a comic sight. Imagine a dark-complexioned little man about four feet ten inches in height, dressed like a tramp with a dirty hat set at an impossible angle, perched on a mule climbing up the mountain path quite oblivious of its rider. He was almost like some modern Sancho Panza for, besides the incongruity, there was at times a wild look in his eyes, a strangeness about him that made his appearance extremely eccentric.

He loved to see the peasant women in their richly embroidered native dress going to church on Sundays along the path with its Stations of the Cross. While we were there he made some beautiful drawings of these women and on his return painted a large picture with scenes of Saas-Fee called *Souvenir of Switzerland*, which I have today and which was, for a long time, on loan to the Tate Gallery, together with a

Souvenir of Switzerland, a detail showing the self-portrait by Stanley Spencer

series of pictures I bought from the Treasury which had been commissioned by the Empire Marketing Board to serve as posters, and which to Stanley's great disappointment had then been stored away in a warehouse and never used.

Stanley was enchanted by the little Swiss villages and chalets and especially the churches with their primitive paintings. On emerging from a church he would stand absorbed in the view to be seen through some arched doorway, built to protect those waiting at the entrance in winter from heavy falls of snow.

He talked with intensity about his work and the way in which he painted. He explained that he liked to photograph a scene in his mind and then reproduce it long afterwards! 'It is much better than if I painted it on the spot because if I feel it sufficiently intensely to paint from memory it has got to live'. For that reason he never really liked his straight landscapes, as he was unable to eliminate any feature, even when he felt that by doing so it would make the design more interesting. Painting from memory enabled him to do this.

Stanley was always pointing out some arresting outline, some combination of colours; and, owing to his ability to see a scene and reproduce it by rethinking it later, his eyes and mind were always alert for effects and ideas. This highly-developed power of observation enabled him to extract what he wanted and paint it later. He was like an animal in a forest, whose eyes are forever on the *qui vive* for a possible quarry.

He used to exclaim 'How marvellous!' about anything done by someone else that he could not do himself; 'How extraordinary the mountaineer who thinks nothing of climbing inaccessible peaks; the mule who can carry loads. . . . I feel like shaking his paw in admiration.' So I told him he might as well shake hands with forty million Frenchmen for being able to talk French. He laughed and said: 'That's just how I feel!'

He spoke of his friend, Henry Lamb, whom he admired as
a painter, a scholar and an excellent pianist, though he fully
recognised that he had less agreeable sides to his nature.
Stanley described an incident before the war, when he was at
the seaside with Lamb and Rupert Brooke and other artists.
Rupert Brooke was very much in love with a girl and wrote
poems to her, and they both behaved as people are supposed
to have done in the romantic period of Byron. Lamb, however, took no account of his feelings and was determined to
have some fun at his expense. He persuaded the girl to let
him spend the night with her — as he said innocently, and
then told Rupert Brooke. Naturally he was very upset, but
Lamb thought it was a splendid joke and pretended he was
saving Rupert Brooke and bringing the two of them to a
sense of reality.

Stanley, too, was sometimes the victim of Lamb's practical
jokes, which apparently were a source of amusement to the
Bloomsbury set — Vanessa Bell, Virginia Woolf, Roger Fry
and their friends.

One day we were walking up a valley and I remarked that
though we would return by the same path, the scenery
would be quite different as we would be seeing it in reverse
— looking at other mountains and new effects of light. He
said: 'Your remark reminds me of an old Persian story I read
some time ago, in which a huntsman was galloping through
a forest and was about to shoot a deer, when he suddenly
realised that he was in a sacred forest and that these were
sacred deer. So he returned slowly through the forest and,
whereas when he was riding headlong in pursuit of game it
had seemed to him a forest just like any other, he suddenly
became aware of the beauty of the scenery, how certain olive
trees were trenched round so that they could be better
irrigated, and he realised the wonderful contrast between
going at full speed and returning at leisure, when all the
beauty of the scenery could be absorbed.'

These allusions to things he had read, or to poetry,

continually occurred in conversations with Stanley. Unlike most people who read a great deal, he only read what interested him and what he read he absorbed completely. He gave me a description of verses by Milton — of how the Devil was pushed back in an encounter, and stood quivering like a mighty mast in a storm, or words to that effect. But the poetry he quoted to explain what he was discussing was suddenly electrified with a kind of pictorial grandeur.

He told me how amused he was by people who tried to explain to him the reasoning behind certain of his paintings. A quite competent artist who had seen the chapel at Burghclere, had discussed at length with him why the crosses in the altar-piece were painted in that particular pattern. To prove his argument he had brought Spencer various designs which he had made of crosses worked into some kind of pattern. Spencer said: 'I never start out with a conscious design. It is the object I am painting which creates the design. In this scene in the chapel, everyone is loving and caressing the crosses as if the men were all in love with the cross, and it is this feeling of devotion which created the design quite unconsciously. No real design is ever worked out like a crossword puzzle.'

Pictorially, he was always seeing something rather terrible in quite simple scenes. 'You see these old houses in this Swiss village and you probably think them beautiful and picturesque. I am rather frightened when I see them because I feel — perhaps quite wrongly — that they are inhabited by dour and surly people who would not like me.' Or again, looking at a particularly clear pool in the mountains, he said: 'There is something really fearful about certain beautiful effects of nature. The purity of this pool is due to the fact that it has never been touched by the hand of man, and therefore, like those glaciers, is something man must guard himself against.'

He told me about his wife; how he had first met her at the house of an artist whose work he praised; how his brother had admired her, and at first he had given way, but then later had himself fallen in love with her because he thought there was some quality in her painting that he could bring out. But he had long since given up this illusion. We had discussed how terrible it is for an artist to marry a woman who had the same interests but a lower artistic standard; how women like that are always jealous of their husband's superiority, and are a hindrance by the very knowledge of his art, instead of being a help.

I said that when I went into his cottage at Cookham and saw the walls covered with his wife's pictures and none by him, I felt I would have liked to throw them all on the rubbish heap. He answered, 'I bet you did!' He mentioned how she disliked being at Burghclere, when he was painting the immense frescoes in the chapel, because people used to say to her, 'How wonderful to be married to such a great artist!', instead of, as she thought, saying how lucky he was to be married to her. She was jealous of his success, and thought little of such friends as myself who enjoyed his company, which she valued lightly. However, he said they had finally come to the conclusion that they were both happier living their own lives. He added that for the past five years he had been fond of a girl called Patricia, a friend of his wife. An entirely platonic relationship that his wife knew about and accepted. (He eventually married her.)

In spite of the fact that Stanley was a particularly unprepossessing man to look at, he always had some woman in his life whom he cared for and who cared for him — generally the type of young old-maid interested in painting. But he told me that on the whole he lived a very lonely life, and rarely found anybody with whom he could have an intellectual conversation or who was sufficiently sympathetic to discuss any subject that came to mind with complete freedom. He was always so modest about himself. 'I feel that my conversation is not interesting because I never meet people, and I am not in touch with what is going on. I feel that I should have to have a whole series of new experiences in life to enable me to talk adequately with people whom I really admire.' He did not realise that the pleasure of talking with him was that he never rehashed the ideas of others. His views were always intensely personal and without any attempt to make an impression.

Talking of Patricia, Stanley mentioned how much she would appreciate the lovely air and Swiss scenery, especially as she had recently been ill; so I arranged for her to come over and join us before I went back to England.

Our last day was perhaps the most memorable of all. They were very happy to be together and I, too, enjoyed being with them.

Stanley walked down part of the way with me, and as we passed the portico of a little church which he admired more than any scenery in the mountains, I remarked to him that it was only fitting we should say goodbye in such a beautiful spot, which we would both remember as a symbol of the delightful days we had spent together.

I often saw Stanley after that. On one occasion a well-known contractor called Charles Boot, who had admired his picture in my house, had given him a commission. He wanted a picture dealing with building activities that he could hang in his office 'showing an avenue of fruit trees in blossom surrounding a building estate in course of completion'. Stanley made two beautiful and interesting pictures, which Boot refused to accept as 'not up to specification'. Boot had no qualms about making a poor artist like Stanley work tirelessly for several months and then not paying him, and I, of course, bought both pictures. One I eventually disposed of through Dudley Tooth. The other, called *The Builders*, was one of his most imaginative creations. I kept it a long time, and during the war lent it, with other pictures of mine, to the Museum of Modern Art in New York and eventually gave it to the Museum.

However, I paid Boot back in his own coin a year later.

I had originally underwritten the capital for his company, but remembering his harsh treatment of Stanley, I refused to underwrite further capital when he again approached me; and he had to abandon a large scheme of development. I would never have minded if a man like Boot had treated me harshly in a business deal: it was all in the usual give and take of my City activities. But at the time I deeply resented his ruthless treatment of a defenceless man like Stanley.

I have recently read Maurice Collis's brilliant book on Stanley. But I think he may have conveyed a wrong impression of the man by quoting so much from letters he never sent and the enormous volume of writings for his secret diary. It is as if his subconscious thoughts or phantasies represented the pattern of his behaviour in life. I do not believe this assumption to be correct.

The last time I met Stanley was at Cookham not long before he died, when he showed me round the exhibition of his works. He was bubbling over with enthusiasm, explaining the meaning of his various pictures and the different people in Cookham he had taken as models to portray some of his biblical subjects. To me he still seemed the innocent, simple person I had known when we first met.

On returning from Switzerland, I took some spacious offices for the new Ocean Trust on the ground floor of Austin Friars, and enjoyed decorating it in a modern attractive manner. We had plenty of business from the start, and all my old City friends gave us a helping hand and we even did several issues jointly with my former firm. When one has worked as a junior to others for many years, there is a great exhilaration in starting up on your own.

About that time I met Isaac Wolfson, and made my first issue for Great Universal Stores (G.U.S.) of a £1,000,000 Debenture, which was to pay for the purchase of businesses today earning several million pounds. I also made an issue on his behalf to acquire the existing capital of Drages. This was for about £1,000,000. He knew the value of the large volume of hire-purchase contracts and how to collect the arrears, and the idea was to purchase and gradually liquidate the business. He had not much spare cash in those days, so I arranged private loans to complete the deal. The investment Trusts were delighted to sell their shares at much over the market price; and I went on the board as chairman, to ensure that jobs were eventually found for all the staff.

In later years I often helped to prepare the Chairman's speech and generally to act as financial adviser to G.U.S. and other Wolfson associated companies. Wolfson was already pursuing his policy of acquiring new businesses for G.U.S. and asked me to approach a mail-order business called Drivers. I took David with me. We arrived at a very dilapidated building in a suburban side street and were ushered into an office, whose wallpaper and shabby furniture was as old as the septuagenarian clerk who asked us to wait a moment. David, who was new to the world of business, said, 'I'm sure we have come to the wrong place, a business earning over £100,000 could not possibly be run in these broken down premises.' It was just because the owner saved every penny and used the minimum of staff that he had built up such a profitable business. Wolfson bought it for around £350,000.

During this period I had an adventure in the Show Ring. While up in Yorkshire on business, by chance I accompanied a friend of mine to a horse sale, and rather recklessly bought what I thought was a wonderful young thoroughbred horse, just over seventeen hands, a bright bay with beautiful conformation. He nearly threw me off the first time I got on his back, as he was very highly-strung, but I was enthused by his looks and paces. I immediately sent him down by horse-box to my friend Sam Marsh, from whom I had bought many fine hunters. He thought highly of the horse and believed it might do well in the shows in the following summer, if I were willing for the horse and its rider to be thoroughly trained. I had never tried my hand at 'showing', and decided I would 'have a go', if only to justify my opinion of the horse, and because, as I have often mentioned before, I liked the idea of adventuring into a new field, if initiated by a chance occurrence.

Sam Marsh is one of the finest riders I have ever known, and even up to a few years ago his skilled and exciting handling of a horse was admired by immense audiences on television. He did a splendid job training the horse, whom we christened Coronation. But it was a harder job training its rider, meaning myself. I had always rather fancied myself as a rider in the hunting-field, or over a modest steeplechase course. But he made me realise I was only an unskilled amateur, when it came to 'showing' or what is now called 'dressage'. This entails putting the horse through all its paces, merely by the gentle pressure of the leg and in response to your voice. Your hands have to be quite still, your position on the horse quiet and correct in every way. And above all, patience, not a natural attribute of mine, was required gradually to coax the horse to obey my voice; just as I had to discipline myself to undergo the necessary training.

It is a lovely human experience if you are able to achieve perfect harmony with your horse. You seem closer to nature and there gradually evolves a feeling that the horse and its rider are one. As Coronation gradually got to understand my wishes, he did all he could to help me. It was not a case of a man 'mastering' a horse. He enjoyed learning new paces, and having a rider on his back able to bring out his best equestrian qualities. I thoroughly enjoyed my apprenticeship with Sam Marsh, who is the complete artist in horsemanship. Weekends at his farm at East Grinstead, early morning rides in Hyde Park, gradually brought improvement.

When summer came, I entered Coronation for a horse show every weekend. How I used to love getting him to stride out in the ring, tail high, ears forward, mane waving, showing off his strength and beauty! I collected numerous cups and medals and finally was delighted to win the Novices'

Heavyweight Hunter Class championships at Olympia. It was great fun, in top hat and pink coat, giving a display in the show-ring at Olympia, the last three nights of the show. But the credit was all due to Sam Marsh for his patient training of horse and rider.

PART TWO

Chapter Eight

★

POLITICAL INTERESTS

THE NATIONAL HOUSING COMMITTEE

THOUGH working hard in the City, I continued to be deeply concerned with public affairs: in the early thirties, in problems of unemployment; and later, when the consequences of the advent of Hitler were played down in governmental circles, with the inadequacy of our defences in the event of war.

Many of us were convinced that a large-scale housing programme would make a valuable contribution to the serious problem of unemployment, for the cost of labour, directly or indirectly, is responsible for 80 per cent of the basic cost of housing. A big housing programme would absorb a large volume of unemployed labour and make a valuable social contribution to the nation's economy. These views are commonplace today, but they were considered very unorthodox at the time.

One man crying out alone in the wilderness can have little influence. But two men equally convinced of the righteousness of a cause can move mountains. I discussed the position with the late B. Seebohm Rowntree, C.H., the chairman of Rowntree, and well-known for his fine humanitarian work; and he was equally enthusiastic. We decided to form a committee called the National Housing Committee, of men well-known for their public services, who would prepare a report on a national housing policy. The gentlemen who agreed to join us on this committee were Lord Amulree (vice-president of the Building Industries National Council), who agreed to act as chairman, Lord Balfour of Burleigh (chairman of the Kensington Housing Committee and later chairman of Lloyds Bank), Sir Basil Blackett (director of the Bank of England), Sir Edgar Bonham-Carter (chairman of the First Garden City, Letchworth), Alfred Bossom (now Lord Bossom, who was vice-chairman of the L.C.C. Housing Committee), Sir Theodore Chambers (chairman of the Rents Tribunal) and Sir Raymond Unwin (president of the Royal Institute of British Architects). We eventually published a report in 1933 advocating that the housing of the lower-paid workers should be accepted as a national responsibility and a public service, and proposing the erection over a period of years of 1,000,000 houses at a rental of ten shillings a week each. (The cost of a house at that time was about £350.)

Through a mutual friend, Sir Anderson Montague-Barlow, I went to see Neville Chamberlain, the minister responsible for these problems. He was courteous and listened politely to the arguments I put forward, but nothing could make him budge from the view that the nation could not afford any large-scale housing policy or any scheme to deal with unemployment that cost money to the Exchequer. I think he regarded me as someone with Bolshevik views. Although I was unsuccessful in persuading the Prime Minister to back our project, the issue of this well-documented report by men of such standing, centred public opinion on the importance of the problem and eventually influenced legislation on the lines suggested in the report. It also provided me with valuable experience as to how future political pressure-groups should be organised. The first thing is to issue a carefully prepared report advocating a certain line of policy, as we did in this case. But a report alone, as I learnt then, is not enough unless backed by the creation of a movement to popularise these views.

THE ARMY LEAGUE

I remembered this experience when dealing with another problem which occurred a few years later. Early in 1937, in view of the likelihood of war, many of us were worried about the inadequate strength of the army, both Regular and Territorial, and the lack of up-to-date equipment. The Regular Army was much below its 1914 strength, and modern equipment for the Territorials was almost non-existent. In fact, on many occasions one could compare summer manœuvres of the Territorial Army to 'flag days', for guns, tanks, armoured cars and even the enemy, were represented merely by coloured flags. Promotion had been so slow that fellow-officers in the Regular Army of my generation who had, like myself, been young battery commanders in the First War, still found themselves with the rank of major twenty years later. Though the British had been the first to invent the tank and had an immense engineering industry, the supply of tanks in quantity and fire-power was negligible.

The Peace Pledge Campaign were conducting a similar movement to that of the Campaign for Nuclear Disarmament today, based on the principle that a disarmed Britain would greatly contribute to preventing war. Supporters of the League of Nations Union, like those of the United Nations now, were urging us to rely on an international organisation to maintain the peace of the world. An influential body of business-men, whose views were often echoed by the Prime Minister, Mr Neville Chamberlain, were in favour of 'business as usual' and shrank from a national effort that would involve increased taxation and the re-orientation of many industries then keyed to profitable peacetime production.

To meet this situation I conceived the idea of forming an Army League, which would play a similar role to the Air League and Navy League for the other two services.

Basing myself on the experience of the National Housing

Committee, I suggested to my friends that we should first get together a committee who would formulate a new policy for the army, to be followed by an active propaganda organisation which would then seek to popularise our proposals.

The Army League Committee was formed under the active chairmanship of L. S. Amery, with myself as deputy chairman. Its members were Sir Anderson Montague-Barlow, former Minister of Labour and whom I had known from my League of Nations days, Captain John Black, of Standard Motors, Captain Victor Cazalet, M.P., Lieutenant-General Sir Ronald Charles, former Director of Military Intelligence at the War Office; Field-Marshal Sir Philip Chetwode, Duncan Sandys, M.P., Sir Harry Hague, owner of Ovaltine, Lord Iliffe, Lord Lloyd, who was president of the Navy League and a great pro-consul, Major R. Macdonald Buchanan, and Field-Marshal Lord Milne, who was formerly Chief of the Imperial General Staff. I drafted the report prepared by this eminent committee.

Some of the older military members of the committee were somewhat nostalgic at what they considered the satisfactory nature of army conditions in their youth. Dear old Lord Chetwode remarked that as a subaltern he had managed all right on his pay of 3/9d a day; but caused great hilarity later when he mentioned that his colonel always came to stay on his estate in Scotland during the grouse shoot!

The report *A Policy for the Army* was finally published in the summer of 1937. It explained the enormous commitments of the army both in case of war on the Continent and overseas, and advocated far-reaching reforms to improve the pay and conditions of service. One of its conclusions might be the echo of conditions at the present moment, for it stated that 'It is necessary that our small army should, in number, be kept at a level commensurate with our vital commitment, be manned by the best type of recruit and be organised with the highest degree of efficiency. . . . The nation must be made to understand the grave risk it is at present exposed to as a result of allowing the strength of the army to fall below the minimum margin of safety. To continue as at present, hoping to muddle through somehow if the danger ever arises, may one day lead this country to irreparable disaster.'

To put over the ideas of the Army League Committee we formed a propaganda body called the Army League, of which I became chairman. We organised a first-class publicity campaign under Richard Temple, the ablest public relations man at that time, to make the contents of the report widely known. The money required was put up privately by some of my City connections and members of our new committee which included, in addition to those who prepared the original report, such well-known personalities as Lord Salisbury, Lord Derby, and Air Marshal Sir John Salmond.

We opened branches all over the country and started a very well illustrated pocket-size monthly magazine called *Rising Strength*, later changed to *Citizen Service*. The magazine gave an account of our campaign in different parts of the country, and included articles showing the development of British preparedness for war throughout the commonwealth. Many of these articles were widely reproduced in the press, stimulated the opening of new Army League branches and, I believe, generally reflected the patriotic reaction to the growing Nazi threats.

Through these activities I became involved, without wishing to be, in some of the internecine squabbles of the Conservative Party. Leslie Hore-Belisha, then Minister of War, who had been a friend since Oxford days, whilst uttering a few nice platitudes about the Army League's activities, did not hide from me personally that he was furious that it diverted publicity from his own plans for army reform. His failure in public life, despite his enormous ability, was due to his egocentric love of personal publicity, and his antagonism to any group who might get reflected praise, however modest, which he considered should always be centred on himself. He did not welcome the Army League's widespread propaganda, and when it advocated greater expenditure on the army than Mr Neville Chamberlain thought prudent, government circles were not slow in suggesting that the movement was getting out of hand. On one occasion I had proposed that Winston Churchill should be a member of our executive committee, but this was turned down flat and not even recorded in the minutes, such was the power of the Conservative government and the 'Establishment' against the independent group of Conservatives who advocated views different from the orthodox opinions of the government. Later, when Leslie had left office, and in his mellowing years, the warmth of our old friendship was renewed and remained so for the rest of his life.

The daily work of the Army League gradually took so much of my time that I had to give up being its chairman. I not only had my business and various directorships, but I had gone back to the army as second-in-command of a London territorial artillery regiment. I had persuaded many of my young City friends to join me; and such was the general enthusiasm to get the best possible training (and the inadequacy of existing facilities) that we used to pay high fees to regular non-commissioned officers to come from Woolwich or Tidworth and teach the troops in their spare evenings and weekends, the only time available for parades. Major-General Sir John Kennedy replaced me as chairman, to be followed later by L. S. Amery, whose energy and wide political experience gave a further great impulse to the League.

Early in 1939, the Army League launched a wider appeal than one solely concerned with army matters. It formed the Citizen Service League, advocating the passing of legislation enforcing 'the principle that the whole youth of the nation, of both sexes, should at about the age of eighteen, receive a

The author, Anthony Eden and George Lowther at a Territorial camp,
Summer 1915

few months training for some service, whether directly connected with defence or otherwise, of national importance in an emergency'. This led to a popular response all over the country, and the last major activity of the Army League before the outbreak of war was to organise a mass-meeting in the Queens Hall, under the chairmanship of L. S. Amery, to advocate compulsory military service.

MISSION TO BULGARIA

From confidential information I had been receiving for some months before the outbreak of war, it seemed to me just possible that Bulgaria might be detached from the Axis. But something had to be done quickly. The entire exports of Bulgaria amounted to only £10 million, chiefly tobacco, with about 20 per cent of fruit and essence of roses used in perfumery. These exports went to Germany, who resold the tobacco, mostly to Scandinavia and the Baltic States; but their monopoly put Bulgaria at the mercy of the Nazis, who at a whim, would leave Bulgarian fruit and tomatoes to rot at railway sidings. The Bulgarians were thus under the economic domination of Germany; if they could be freed from this, there was a chance of their escaping from Axis domination. Though Rumania and Greece were favourable to Britain, these two allies were neutralised by the position of Bulgaria. If Bulgaria could be won over, the Balkans might form a solid block against the Axis.

With recommendations from the Foreign Office, my partner David Long and I flew to Sofia. Our ambassador, Sir George Rendel, was enthusiastic about my proposals, as his recommendations to the government had met with no response.

Germany's ruthless and arrogant policies had antagonised Bulgaria, where leading newspapers were still in the French language, and the Bulgarian peasants revered Russia as their former liberator from Turkish oppression. Sir George considered that Bulgaria might be detached if she were to receive economic aid from the Allies, who would also have to use their influence to persuade Rumania to return Southern Dobrudga, a small territory populated almost solely by Bulgarians, and ceded during a recent Balkan war.

In Sofia I met the Prime Minister and most members of the cabinet, and a contract was finally signed by which the Ocean Trust would be the export agents of the government. This agreement did not entail any profit for the Ocean Trust, but was conceived as a suitable procedure for helping to divert Bulgarian exports away from Axis countries. As American tobacco companies mix 'Turkish-type' tobacco with their Virginian leaf, I arranged to go to New York, taking with me a Bulgarian delegation representing the tobacco co-operatives, with a view to negotiating increased purchases by the American tobacco companies, who had been previously approached. I also hoped to arrange for a British canning company to put up a small factory to can Bulgarian tomatoes and fruits and make Bulgaria less dependent on exports to Germany. Also it was important to persuade British shipping companies to call more often at Bulgarian ports, on their way to and from Balkan and Turkish territory; it was a case of enlightened co-operation.

Various members of the Bulgarian government explained to me that none of them had personal means outside their small salaries and that if they stood up against the Germans, and King Boris, and their action proved unsuccessful, they might be left penniless. They asked me if it would be possible to provide them with a small sum like £500 or £1000 a year in a safe currency abroad, in case they were thrown out of office, so that they could provide for their families.

The Bulgarians are a hard-working, frugal, peasant population. There was hardly any industry in the country and the standard of living was very modest, so that £1000 a year was considered a high salary at that time.

When I got back to London, I prepared a detailed report

for Lord Halifax, which was warmly endorsed by Sir George Rendel. I also went to see Mr Neville Chamberlain, and pointed out the great advantages that could be gained by bringing Bulgaria over to our side, and the comparatively small cost. The total exports of the country, even if purchased and thrown into the sea, would be a small price to pay compared with the political advantages. All that was necessary was to do as the Germans did, buy the crops and gradually resell them to other countries. I said I felt confident of being able to place a large part of their tobacco crop with the Americans; and the government might persuade the British tobacco companies that it was in 'the national interest' to purchase small quantities of Bulgarian tobacco. And as for giving security to members of the Bulgarian cabinet, £100,000 would cover the lot.

Mr Neville Chamberlain strongly disapproved of my suggestions, saying that Bulgaria was 'in the natural economic orbit of Germany, and to try to divert her trade away would be one of the circumstances that might precipitate a world war'. As for what he called offering a small financial security to members of the Bulgarian government, this was just bribery and no government under his leadership could countenance it. Well, there it was. It was the same kind of language I had heard when I had advocated a national housing policy. As for the financial amounts involved, it was a mere trickle compared with the enormous sums soon to be expended by the Ministry of Economic Warfare, for similar purposes.

War was declared a few weeks later as I arrived in New York, with the Bulgarian agricultural delegation, and this of course put an end to my negotiations.

I flew back in a special private plane, as my old friend, Lord Lothian, our ambassador, making me a King's Messenger for the journey, had entrusted me with a personal letter from President Roosevelt to Mr Neville Chamberlain.

I spent my last evening in New York with Willie Wiseman[1] and Johnnie Schiff, who by then had become senior partner of the American banking firm of Kuhn Loeb. I had often met Johnnie out hunting, so I told him, as I would be rejoining my regiment, I would give him my three hunters and arrange for them to be sent over immediately on my return to England. He was delighted. The horses were marvellous performers and had given me many happy days with the Pytchley. I was pleased to think they would be well cared for and do credit to themselves jumping over the high railed fences of the Long Island hunt.

[1] The late Sir William Wiseman, Bart.

Chapter Nine

★

DUNKIRK

O N MY return home I closed down the Ocean Trust and rejoined my regiment. I found it quite a hard job learning and teaching the new artillery technique.

Three months later I was summoned to the War Office and told I had been appointed to a staff job at G.H.Q. in France, in the operations branch. I asked where G.H.Q. was situated, and was told this was a Top Secret but that I would get the information from the R.T.O. (Railway Transport Officer) on my arrival in Calais.

Unfortunately there was a violent storm in the Channel and the boat arrived hours late, so when I went to look for the R.T.O. he was nowhere to be found. However, outside the station several taxis were plying for hire and, to my surprise, one of the drivers shouted out 'Gee Hash Queux'. 'Do you know where it is?', I asked in astonishment. 'Of course, at Arras. Five-hundred francs.' When we got to the old town, which brought back so many memories of the previous war, he asked me, '*Opérations ou Administration?*' I replied '*Opérations*', whereupon he drove straight to the Hôtel de Ville. It was a cold winter and not a leaf remained on any of the forlorn-looking trees on the square opposite, but under each tree stood a number of staff cars. There was no sentry outside headquarters, but as I came inside the door I was greeted by a terrific salute from one of the tallest guardsmen I can remember. I asked for General Lord Gort, to whom I was to report, but was told he was out. I therefore reported to General Mason-MacFarlane, head of Military Intelligence, formerly our military attaché in Berlin, whom I had met on many occasions. He asked me how I had managed to get there, as they had sent a car to fetch me at Calais, but it had returned empty. When I told him my story he threw up his arms in horror, exclaiming '*There has been a terrible leak*'. Apparently it was thought that no one would know where our G.H.Q. was situated if there was no guard at the entrance, and the many cars standing outside were 'camouflaged' under the leafless trees!

Being at G.H.Q. was a pleasant change from dull regimental routine. In the operations room I was briefed on the order of battle of the British and French armies and the general tactical and strategic situation. Soon I was posted as one of the twelve British liaison-officers (nicknamed the Twelve Apostles), with the French army; these included two old city friends, Colonel Rex Benson, and Koch de Goyrend. I was attached to the French road transport section in Amiens, which directed the movement of the whole French army. My staff consisted of one captain, one lieutenant and a few N.C.O.s, and under the French we managed to direct the movements of the six divisions of the British army.

What surprised me was the very small number of staff used by the French, compared to British standards: one colonel, a captain, and two junior officers controlled the movements of 110 French divisions. It was mostly done by telephone, with the minimum of written orders; and it all seemed to work very smoothly. There was no separate road transport section in the British army, whose tactical thinking was still largely based on the technique of trench-warfare of the last war. Because new regulations had enforced the principle of leaving a large gap between vehicles, as a defence against air attack, it took nearly a day for a division to pass a given point, and the problem of moving divisions

The author, 1940

in different directions without careful co-ordination at the
highest level, and road patrols at key-points, was a very real
one. We soon had a practical example of the need for a
transport-control section when a forlorn general arrived at
Arras, having lost his division. This created much amusement
at G.H.Q., and solicitous young staff-officers kept coming
in to enquire, in sympathetic tones, of the general, whether
his division had turned up. It had disembarked at Cher-
bourg and was due up near the Belgian frontier, but had
been missing for twenty-four hours. We later heard that a
lieutenant in one of the leading units had taken the wrong
turning in a village and gone due south instead of north-
east, and the whole division had followed him.

I sent in long reports advocating that we should form a
road section in the British army and this was supported by
G.H.Q., but the idea was held up by the establishment
committees of the War Office, who had to work out the
problems of what its personnel should be. If so many men
were required, then there would have to be a corresponding
number of N.C.O.s, drivers and cooks. The problem had
not yet been solved when the Germans finally attacked.

The French officers of my group hated going to our
G.H.Q., as Lord Gort, remembering the criticism against
staff extravagance in the First War, went to the other
extreme, and the mess there consisted largely of army
rations such as bully beef and army biscuits. In contrast the
French 'popote', of even quite small units, was always
excellent.

When the Duke of Gloucester inspected our defensive
positions on the Belgian frontier, I was posted to his staff.
I was surprised to find that no Maginot line existed along the
Franco-Belgian frontier, but only a line we had built ourselves consisting of barbed-wire entanglements, protected
by small pill-boxes, which seemed a most amateur affair. In
fact, what worried me was to discover the total lack of
modern equipment and the small number of anti-tank guns

I

available. The army had a rather good heavy anti-tank rifle, which would pierce most light tanks, but there were only thirty rounds of ammunition per rifle available. The rifle gave a nasty kick until one became accustomed to it, and it needed more than thirty rounds for practice purposes before anyone could be sufficiently confident to use it in battle.

On my first leave I went to see Mr Leslie Burgin, the new Minister of Supply. I emphasised the dangers that might arise from the serious deficiencies in essential weapons, and offered to come and help at the Ministry for a short period to get things started, since I felt sure I could be spared from my modest job in the army for this purpose. He knew of my industrial and administrative experience, as we had often met in the past on business matters. He said he would think it over, and arranged an appointment for two days later. When he saw me again he said he believed I might be able to help, but added, 'What I have to consider is my political position. Quite confidentially as man to man, how can I be certain that you are not acting as a spy for General Gort?' I blushed for shame that a member of the government in wartime should ask such a question of a serving soldier, about his commander-in-chief. In a fury I replied that if that was how he felt about the war, I would not dream of working for him, and left without shaking hands. The episode showed how urgently Winston Churchill was needed at the helm.

When I got back to G.H.Q. I asked to be allowed to return to regimental duties, as I was forty-three, and would not be eligible for promotion to lieutenant-colonel without a further period with a regiment. Before I left Amiens one of my friends on G.H.Q. at Arras begged me to help him to wangle my job. What could be better he said than living in Amiens at the Hôtel du Rhin, within such easy reach of Paris and being your own boss! Alas, he did not long enjoy the comfortable time he hoped for. Apparently a month or so later the concierge rushed up to him in the early hours one morning and told him he had heard that German tanks were entering Amiens. 'These Frenchmen always panic!' he exclaimed, as he turned over to go back to sleep; 'Don't forget to bring me chocolate and croissants punctually at eight.' At eight o'clock he was awakened by a German orderly and he spent the rest of the war in a prison camp. Our Intelligence heard these sad details later from his orderly, who had escaped in time.

I was posted as second-in-command of the 32nd Field Regiment, a regular artillery regiment, then training around Lille. Our brigadier was Robin Staveley, who had been my battery commander in the first war. The regiment was a splendid unit that had just returned from India.

On a fine summer's day the 'balloon went up' and war started in earnest. We were ordered to move through Belgium, in accordance with one of the many prepared plans I had studied in so much detail at G.H.Q. As we crossed the Belgian frontier, our regiment was greeted with cheers and flowers from an enthusiastic populace. 'The British are coming to save us, all will be well.' My feelings were not so jubilant. I knew something of our strategic plans and weaknesses.

We gradually moved forward to Brussels, meeting battered remnants of the forward Belgian army, as well as droves of refugees on the roads. My regiment took part in supporting Montgomery's 3rd Division's gallant counter-attack at Louvain, and then the general retreat was ordered.

My regiment was left on the canal-bank outside Brussels, with orders to fire a number of rounds at fixed targets when the enemy approached Brussels, and then rejoin our main forces, which had already evacuated the Belgian capital. It was quite eerie when all the army had left, having blown up the bridges over the canal. We kept the motors of our vehicles running while we waited for the Germans to appear. Then we somehow managed to fire the required number of volleys and escape without casualties, racing along the deserted roads until at last we rejoined the bulk of our forces near Alost.

Later that day my colonel was wounded and I took over command of the regiment. This time I had none of that carefree feeling of the previous war. In a retreat every mistake is paid for. There is no second chance. I had very often to decide on the tactical position without orders; and had continually to reconnoitre new alternative positions to retreat to. On one occasion I was so tired I just could not focus properly to take a reading on my compass. I told my orderly to wake me up in twenty minutes and lay down and went straight to sleep. When I woke up I was completely restored.

It often happens in a defensive battle that when you have made every possible preparation, all you can do is wait, in anxiety and apprehension, until the enemy decides to attack. In the lull I started to read my pocket edition of Plato's *Symposium*. This discussion between Socrates and his friends on the meaning of love and friendship represents to me all that is most noble and civilised in man. Soon I began to feel quite calm and detached.

Our retreating army was losing its orderly cohesion, and it became more and more difficult to know what was the position on one's flanks. So one morning, hoping to get some up-to-date news, I chased down on my motor-bike to the temporary location of our ever-moving Corps headquarters. To my surprise it was being shelled, without much effect, by a solitary German tank.

In the midst of the confusion I went into the Operations room and on a desk saw a G.H.Q. operation order stating that the British Expeditionary Force would retreat to Dunkirk, destroy all its equipment and evacuate by sea to England. Then followed some twenty pages of red and blue type with illustrations showing different methods of blowing up and destroying equipment. I asked the staff-officer on duty if this was correct, and he confirmed that these were the orders that had just been received.

I went back at full speed to inform my divisional general of the G.H.Q. orders I had seen. He refused to believe me, exclaiming, 'The British army would never do a thing like that, leaving its allies in the lurch, and scuttling back to England.' Nothing I could say would convince him, and Corps H.Q. was on the move again, so he could get no confirmation or denial of what I had told him.

When I left I thought to myself what a silly old man, but when I reflected on the situation weeks later, it came to me that there must be real strength in a country whose soldiers cannot believe they can ever be defeated.

We fought a gruelling rearguard action that afternoon at Hazebrouck, which I had known so well in the last war. At ten o'clock that night we had orders to support a large counter-attack next morning, four miles east of Hazebrouck, but I pointed out that all that was left of the Hazebrouck troops was about a company resting with us well to the west of the town, which was now in enemy hands, and that our present gun position was the front line.

At four o'clock in the morning came the order to retreat exactly as I had seen it at eleven o'clock the previous morning at Corps H.Q., except that it left discretion of the line of retreat to each unit. It had taken fifteen hours for the orders to be conveyed from Corps, owing to the clerks on the staff having had to roneo in two colours the long description of the various methods of destroying equipment. This meant we had to start our retirement in daylight in full view of the enemy.

We had many adventures on our way to Dunkirk, attached to different divisions, or newly-created groups, or sometimes fighting unattached in support of the nearest infantry unit. At one time, reconnoitring in advance of the regiment near Mont Kemmel, driving east, I came in contact with a German patrol. I quickly drove in the opposite direction and met some German tanks twelve miles away. If the Germans had only known, they could have sealed off the bulk of our Expeditionary Force now moving north, facing the enemy to east and west, along a corridor at times hardly twenty miles wide. I was much more frightened than I had been as a young man, though my habit of going for a run every day during our training period had helped to keep me fit for the present ordeal. My former battle experience also came in useful. In a retreat bad news is repeated and magnified. 'The Germans have just occupied so and so,' a panicky soldier would exclaim. 'Did you see them yourself?' 'No, but I was told, Sir.' 'Then don't believe it.'

I have never been so proud in all my life as I was to be a member of this small retreating army. I knew personally, or by sight, from school, university, the City, the previous war, perhaps as many as a quarter of its officers. And the spirit of the army was that if this was to be Britain's last battle, then each unit would vie with the other to prove worthy of its most glorious traditions. The cooks, the clerks, the so-called tail of the army, hurriedly mustered together into small groups, fought as courageously as the well-known regiments of the line.

As we reached the perimeter of Dunkirk we were met by first-class staff organisation. Guides directed us to large fields where our guns and vehicles were carefully parked in line. The long memorandum roneo'd in two colours by G.H.Q. and Corps H.Q. had not been necessary after all, for the enemy eventually captured all this immense amount of equipment, parked with careful military precision.

The Press has always made Dunkirk out as a terrible ordeal. I did not feel that way. After fighting rearguard actions all the way there, with the awesome thought that one might get surrounded and taken prisoner, Dunkirk, with ships waiting to take us back to England, was the promised land!

I had a wonderful feeling marching at the head of the remnants of the regiment, carrying all our light equipment, rifles and machine-guns through the burning town of Dunkirk. The men too felt elated, as if we had won a victory.

Pictorially, Dunkirk was a scene of dramatic beauty that I will never forget. The burning oil-tankers poured a dense cloud of smoke over the town, broken by the flames of sharp bursts of anti-aircraft guns firing point-blank at diving enemy planes; and the many burning houses made a reddish glow in the sky. It was raining as we reached the seafront, and the rain had dampened the burning woodwork of the Casino, making it look like the set-piece of a giant firework display. Sunken ships were upturned in the harbour.

It was almost dark as I moved slowly with the crowd of soldiers along the mole to board the destroyer. From time to time I looked back at the amazing scene we were leaving behind, and the thought came to me that I was living through a great moment in our history. As the destroyer moved off, I fell fast asleep on a coil of rope on the top deck, too exhausted to heed the pouring rain or the mass of men around me.

Chapter Ten

1942 ONWARDS

AFTER Dunkirk my military activities were confined to soldiering in England. My old friend Colin Gubbins, by then a Major-General, was organising localised guerrilla-warfare units to meet the eventuality of a possible invasion of Britain, and I joined him, only returning to my regiment when the threat had passed.

One of my great joys, when on leave, was to go and stay with Violet and Sydney.

They had always been searching for a 'perfect' home in the country, and, as I have already told, had lived in many places. At last they found a small Elizabethan manor in the little village of Abinger Common on Leith Hill in Surrey. Here, from about 1930 they made their home, although they often moved back to their house in Kensington for short periods.

It goes without saying that Abinger soon became a centre for their many friends, young and old. There Sydney, with his creative energy and love of nature, made another beautiful garden, and among many improvements, turned the old garage and barn into a charming modern cottage for guests. Here, when they left their home in Rapallo, Max Beerbohm and his wife Florence stayed during the first four years of the war.

Since they were such close neighbours, Sydney and Max made the most elaborate plans to avoid getting in each other's way. There was to be no communication except by letter, the telephone was taboo, no talking over the hedge,

Sydney and Max, by Max Beerbohm

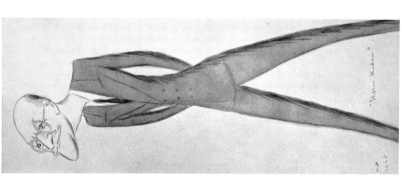

Sydney, by Max Beerbohm

visits were formal and announced in advance by letter, either slid under the door, or through the letterbox. These letters assumed more and more importance in their daily lives during the isolation of the war years, and were a source of endless amusement. 'Thank Heaven that even Hitler cannot drive laughter out of Europe', wrote Max one day. Sometimes Max would set about 'improving' the advertisements in a newspaper in his own inimitable way, adding a skirt or a hat here, and a leg there, invent appropriate captions, and then slide it under the Schiffs' front-door. Later in the day it would probably come back with comments or a story added.

The two men also kept up a continuous correspondence on various subjects, and the surreptitious delivery of these epistles, their author tiptoeing away from the door and sometimes meeting unexpectedly with his friend on the mat outside, was not without an element of adventure and excitement.

There was only fifty yards between the two houses, which were separated by a hedge and low wall with a path alongside, and there the two men would spend hours walking up and down in earnest conversation, muffled up to the ears in winter in their thick overcoats, hats well pulled down, and in summer dressed in the light-grey or lavender suits they both loved to wear, for they were tremendous dandies.[1] If I arrived while they were having one of their 'constitutionals' I would hurry out to join them, and in any case I often crossed the 'frontier' to visit Max and Florence and to listen to Max's version of the never-ending interchange between the two households.

Having nowhere to put my many pictures during the war, I had put some on the walls of the cottage. This enticed Max, with his vivid imagination, to make caricatures of the people they portrayed, which were often accompanied by a 'secret' history of their lives.

[1] See the illustration facing this page.

On one occasion when I turned up in Abinger I found the subject of the amusing daily exchanges was the discovery of a rat in the cottage! After many letters had passed between them, Max wrote to Sydney, '*All* precautions will be taken for the discouragement of any possible advent of another rat! I may even go so far as to go to London and order the costume of the Pied Piper.' Another time Max told me one of his typical anecdotes: 'I heard a sad story the other day about a man who went to consult a nerve specialist. He said, "One of the things that worry me, and make me afraid, is that when I'm alone I can't help talking to myself." "Oh well", said the consultant, "many people do that. It's not at all a dangerous sign." The patient, leaning forward, said, "But, Doctor, *I'm such an awful bore.*" '

On another occasion Max sent Violet and Sydney a rather sad new poem by T. S. Eliot called *East Coker*, which Max summarised as follows:

> Wot's the good o' trying to earn a living nowadays?
> Wot's the good of enythink when 'umbug only pays?
> Wot's the good o' shaving?
> Or of raving about saving?
> Wot's the good of *enythink*? Why, *nothink*!

Being with Violet and Sydney, and having talks with Max and Florence, was a delightful escape from dreary regimental routine.

In 1942 the army, having decided to reduce the age of its regimental commanders in the field, gave me the alternative of retiring or of training troops at home; so I decided to retire. But I had nostalgic regrets when at Dorchester my regiment marched past on my last parade. It was like saying goodbye to youth, to memories of gallant comrades and to a sense of adventure. And I also had a feeling of personal failure.

Immediately on leaving the army I set about planning new activities. I restarted the Ocean Trust, but was determined that henceforth its financial side should not overshadow my greater interest in managing industrial undertakings and playing a major part in their development.

To further the war effort my first venture was an engineering factory at Acton. It made components for the aeroplane and electronic industries. I was lucky enough to secure the technical assistance of Robert C. Cox, one of the finest engineers in the country. Henceforth he was my partner in most of my engineering projects. Quite early I had learned how important it is, in any industrial or commercial venture, to get to know your personal deficiencies and then to compensate for this lack of knowledge by selecting capable specialists or technicians. This then constitutes a team which, if wisely chosen, is a combination far superior to the dictatorial superman.

At that time the engineering industry was working fifty-six hours a week, which was a great personal hardship for the employees, who had to travel to and from work in the blackout, often during air-raids. Despite preliminary opposition from the Ministry of Supply, working hours at my Acton factory were considerably reduced and we found this resulted in increased production and efficiency.

In the City I received a special welcome from my old friends, Mr Walter Whigham of Robert Fleming, Mr A. H. Wynn of the Mercantile Investment Trust, Mr Crump of the Prudential Assurance, Mr Stride of the Industrial and General Trust, and Mr Harley Drayton of Securities Agency. With them the Ocean Trust formed a syndicate to purchase the old Monmouthshire brewery business of Webbs (Aberbeeg) Limited, of which I became chairman.

Not being a beer-drinker myself, I thought it might be a good idea to develop other sides of the beverage business, so one hot summer's day I went down to Devon to negotiate the purchase of a well-known cider firm. I was welcomed by the owner, Mr Ridler, a rugged-looking farmer nearing seventy, with old-fashioned side-whiskers and a finely-weathered face. He and his son suggested that before we got down to discussing terms, I should be refreshed with some ice-cold 'home brew'. It was a wonderful drink and I had several large glasses before, in my innocence, I discovered its potent effects, for the 'home brew' is several times stronger in alcoholic content than any commercial cider. The Ridlers, in consequence, made a better bargain than they had expected, with a buyer who was having great difficulty in remaining steady on his feet. Through internal development and amalgamations, the profits of Webbs rose from £28,000 in 1942 to over £200,000 by the time I eventually retired from the chairmanship some years after that.

Later the Ocean Trust, in conjunction with the same group, bought the worsted-spinning business of Jeremiah Ambler Limited, in Bradford, founded in the late eighteenth century. It was an old family business, run by trustees, for descendants of the original founders. The existing shareholders, who took no part in the management of the business, were always bringing pressure on the trustees to pay out as much as possible in dividends, and were unable to provide the further finance required for modernisation and development, and to face the risks involved in such a policy.

The mills had been partly 'concentrated' during the war, and were not working to capacity. To take over a business of this kind was quite a challenge, but I was lucky enough to have my old friend Lord Barnby, with a lifetime's experience in the wool and textile industry, to help me on the technical side. I also liked the idea of trying to build up a concern in Bradford, to which my family had emigrated from Germany after the Napoleonic wars. I am still chairman of Ambler's today, and its profits have risen from a modest £35,000 in 1944 to well over £400,000 at the present time.

I have always noticed that industrial trends in America, the most highly industrialised country in the world, are followed a number of years later in Great Britain. So when the war was ending I went to the United States to examine new industrial developments, and find out if new products developed there during the war might be suitable for manufacture in Britain.

In this way I secured the manufacturing and selling rights of the Bendix washing-machine in Britain and the British Empire. In the States an automatic washing-machine was becoming a top priority, and I chose the Bendix washing-machine because a million had already been sold and, therefore, the technical difficulties had been well ironed out.

When I returned to England I tried to find a partner in this venture and discussed it with my friend Isaac Wolfson. Up to that time only the most rudimentary washing-machines had been sold in this country, and Wolfson said he could not foresee a demand for an expensive automatic machine, as the public was not yet washing-machine-minded. There was also the problem of manufacture. For this purpose I contacted Fisher & Ludlow, one of the largest makers of motor bodies, who were looking out for new post-war products. They joined me in developing the Bendix, and I became chairman of Fisher & Ludlow as well as chairman and managing-director of the newly-created Bendix Home Appliances.

The manufacture of the Bendix was not easy, as the mass-production of large home appliances in Great Britain was in its infancy. For instance, the machine has a time-switch for controlling the change-over from soaking to rinsing, requiring a change every three minutes. The only time-switches I could obtain were from high-precision clock manufacturers, who would guarantee an exactitude of within a second a week. This was much too expensive, as such high precision was not required and the efficiency of the washing operation was not impaired if the mechanism was two or three seconds out for a three-minute cycle.

To be able to sell the machine at a reasonably low price it was necessary to devise means for starting straight away on large-scale production. We got together a first-class team of specialist salesmen, experienced in selling and servicing refrigerators. We then bought twelve American machines which were shown at the Ideal Home Exhibition, trade fairs and other exhibitions. Through demonstrations of our twelve American machines, we obtained advance orders for the home market as well as for Australia and New Zealand for about 25,000 machines, before the start of actual production. Bendix Home Appliances were thus immediately enabled to give Fisher & Ludlow a large production order. The success of the machine in the first year might have induced us to go out for a large profit per machine, but we were quite content to make a profit of around £5 per machine selling at about £85, so as not to excite competition, and maintain a large volume of sales. The first year's sales were nearly £2,000,000.

I started to introduce in my own factories the idea of having Bendix washing-machines installed as a welfare contribution. Women would leave their washing in the morning and collect it in the evening, when it would be washed and dried ready to take home. This was greatly appreciated, and is today quite a regular feature in factories employing a lot of women.

We also started the system of laundry shops called Launderettes, which has now spread all over the country. This opened a new avenue for selling machines. It was also a useful advertisement, as many people would graduate from using a Bendix machine in a Launderette, to wanting to purchase one of their own.

Though I became chairman of Fisher & Ludlow because of the Bendix, the production of the Bendix machine was quite a minor side of its business activities. When I joined the company, I found that its production was spread out in small factories all over Birmingham, which made it extremely difficult to arrange meetings of the executives at short notice. As a result we made a decision to take over, on a rental basis, the 2,000,000 square feet of factory space at Castle Bromwich, which was one of the splendid new factories built at a cost of £3½ million by the government for wartime production and which was now redundant. The successful operation of transferring to a new factory without disturbing existing mass-production was a tribute to the technical and organising skill of the Fisher & Ludlow staff, for the machinery included hundreds of presses weighing up to one hundred tons each. The change-over to Castle Bromwich greatly helped the business; the company made a capital profit of £500,000 in selling its old factories, and the Ocean Trust made an issue of £1,000,000 4-per-cent Unsecured Notes to provide extra working capital for the greatly enlarged production.

One of the difficulties I first met at Fisher & Ludlow was to get the engineering directors to agree to increasing the salaries of certain key managers. They would think nothing of agreeing to buy a few new presses at £30,000 each, but to increase an engineer's salary by £500 a year took a great deal of persuasion on my part. My American experience had strengthened my belief in high salaries, and bonus payments for key men.

Being chairman of Fisher & Ludlow was at times almost a full-time job. We had difficult negotiations with the leading motor-car companies on new models, and labour controversy was acute when new cars went into production; there was also continuous controversy with the Ministry of Supply to get sufficient allocation of steel to plan production. I very much enjoyed dealing with these problems, where so much depended on the success of personal discussions with the people involved.

During this period I also became chairman of Gray's Carpets and Textiles, a group which Isaac Wolfson had amalgamated after the war, to supply the needs of his Great Universal Stores. Not long after Gray's became a public company, its sales to G.U.S. were greatly diminished. The high rate of purchase-tax hit its worsted-weaving and Irish-linen companies which made top-quality goods; and its cotton production suffered from the competition of heavy imports from the East. This was the only public company of which I was chairman that was not successful during my chairmanship. I think perhaps I was over-optimistic at the start, and when business conditions changed adversely I was not quick enough in cutting out the dead wood. I am glad to say that under an able new chairman, who was my colleague for many years, the company is now making a successful recovery.

Chapter Eleven

★

MAKING PUBLIC ISSUES AND INVESTMENT PROBLEMS

ONE advantage I had in helping to develop industrial companies of which I was a director, was that owing to my financial experience, the question of finding further capital did not usually present difficulties. Nevertheless, making issues of capital to the public is a very skilled affair. In each boom new personalities come into prominence in this type of business, but many fall by the wayside when more difficult times approach. Today, strict scrutiny by the Stock Exchange of every prospectus prevents obvious pitfalls and the frauds that occurred when less stringent regulations were in force; but no regulations can provide the right kind of financial foresight on behalf of the issuing house itself.

The first thing an issuing house aims to do is to spot the 'winners' of the future, in the form of owners of good private companies that decide to 'go public'. 80-per-cent death-duties and enormous surtax force most owners of private companies, at a certain stage of their development, to turn themselves into a public company; for if 25 per cent of the shares of a public company are held by outside shareholders, the company is no longer subject to surtax. If a private company can prove to the Inland Revenue that it needs to keep its cash in the business because of development, it can avoid surtax direction for quite a time. Some private companies, to avoid surtax, have continually bought new businesses with overdrafts from the banks. To purchase a new business as a means of avoiding surtax, unless it fits in

K

well with the activities of a parent company, may prove
dangerous. The recent credit-squeeze has dealt a hard blow
to certain private companies associated with the motor and
home-appliance businesses who, instead of having reserves
of liquid capital in hand to meet a rainy day, have over-
extended themselves to avoid surtax and find themselves called
upon to repay bank loans under adverse trading conditions.

Having so often had to advise companies in this situation,
I have on occasion agreed with the old saying that banks
lend you money as people lend you an umbrella when the
sun is shining, and want it back when it starts to rain. As
I have already explained, Sir Montague Burton nearly lost
control of his business because of pressure from one of the
joint-stock banks. The same thing happened in the case of the
now famous store of Simpson (Piccadilly) Limited. Simpson
Limited, wholesale clothiers and the makers of Daks
trousers, was an old-established firm, showing an average
earning of about £90,000 for the previous twenty years. It
was owned by the Simpson family, and under the management of Alec Simpson, then in his early thirties. He decided
to enlarge the scope of the undertaking by opening a store
in Piccadilly, both to increase its turnover and advertise its
products. Their bank willingly offered the overdraft
facilities required, and Alec Simpson imagined he was free
from financial worries. £200,000 had been spent in buying
the site and erecting the bare walls of the building, when
suddenly the bank refused further credit. Dollfuss had just
been assassinated and the international political situation
was tense. As always in such cases, the bank explains to the
client, who previously had thought his overdraft was a
generously given long-term credit, that of course the bank
is only the trustee for the deposits of others and 'in the
circumstances. . . .' This was disastrous as the store had to
be filled with goods, and it takes two to three years for any
large departmental store to make a profit, for, unlike a
multiple shop which can earn profits in the first year, it needs

time for a store to build up a large enough habitual clientele.

Lord Barnby told me of this situation, and I was so impressed with Alec Simpson's dynamic and go-ahead personality that I decided to try to find the finance necessary to save him. It was no longer a matter of business but of principle to see him through. I went to the leading investment trusts and insurance companies and managed to convince them of the soundness of the business and the unfairness of the position. I was thus able to place privately £200,000 4¾-per-cent Debentures and £200,000 5½-per-cent Notes secured on the building and guaranteed by S. Simpson Ltd., the parent company. This enabled the bank to be repaid (to their surprise) and provided £200,000 to meet the cost of further development. These two issues were made at ½-per-cent higher rate of interest than was current at the time. But that is the right way to force through the provision of additional finance in difficult circumstances. The extra interest cost the company an additional £2,000 a year, less tax, but saved the business which, in 1961, earned over £300,000. Lord Barnby went on the Board to help Alec Simpson with the benefit of his wider business experience. Alas, young Alec Simpson died of cancer a few years after the store had been opened; and the business then came under the control of his brother, an able Harley Street doctor.

It is usual, as I have explained in an earlier chapter, quoting the case of Lord Camrose, that companies who have been helped in their formative period, continue with the same issuing house in after years. But gratitude is a rare quality and I was not surprised when fifteen years later I read in the newspapers that another firm had placed the Ordinary shares of Simpson (Piccadilly) Limited on the market.

As I have already mentioned, it is often better to follow the man than the industry. In doing so it may happen that you are ahead of public opinion at the time. I found the original finance for men like Sir Montague Burton, Sir

Richard Fairey, E. K. Cole, Sir Isaac Wolfson, Charles Clore, Maxwell Joseph, Charles Forte and many others, who when they started were often called 'dangerous' and 'speculators', as are most successful young business-men at the beginning of their careers.

Having decided on the business, the issuing house must next decide on the right financial plan. This is generally the most difficult thing of all. It must be a plan that will meet the immediate financial needs of the company. The capitalisation must also be sufficiently elastic to provide for future developments or the avenues of new finance may be blocked. When I first discussed the position of Associated British Pictures with John Maxwell, its chairman and founder, he told me the immediate financial requirements of the company were £1,750,000. When we examined the programme, it was obvious that he would need £3,500,000 within two years to be safe. So we decided on an immediate issue of £2,500,000 Debentures at a slightly higher rate of interest, with an authorised amount of £3,500,000, so that a further £1,000,000 could be issued later.

My first issue for Isaac Wolfson was in 1938, in the form of £1,000,000 4½-per-cent Debenture for Great Universal Stores. This was secured on all the freehold and other assets of the company. These were the best terms I could secure for the company at the time, but a provision in the Debenture deed gave the company, if it prospered, the right to repay the Debentures at a small premium. This debenture was redeemed after the war by the issue of a 4-per-cent Preference share, thus leaving all the properties free of mortgage.

The issuing house should also try to ensure, as far as possible, that any securities offered to the public or to the shareholders of the company will meet with a ready response, or are, in other words, 'oversubscribed'. Mossy Myers, on occasion, erred in his natural desire to help his client, in making the terms of the issue on too narrow a margin to be always successful. This is bad for the company concerned, as it harms its financial credit with the City and the public, and may prove expensive in the long run. The first time Charles Clore made an issue for Sears after the war, it was a £2,000,000 5-per-cent Debenture. The Ocean Trust made this issue in 1954, jointly with Harley Drayton's Securities Agency Limited, and the brokers were Cazenove and Sebags. I was told that with luck we might get away with a 4¾-per-cent Debenture, but I stuck out for a 5-per-cent Debenture issued at 100 per cent, to ensure an overwhelming success for Clore, who had at that time been criticised for his pioneering take-over-bid tactics.

In 1948 the Ocean Trust had underwritten a £1,000,000 3¼-per-cent Debenture issue for the Ericsson Telephone Company, but just before the printing of the prospectus there had been a sudden fall in the gilt-edged market. I explained the position fully to Sir Harold Wernher, the chairman of Ericsson who, despite the fact that the issue at 3¼ per cent had been fully underwritten, agreed to increase the rate to 3½ per cent. The issue was a great success; and today a rate of 3½ per cent does not seem a high rate of interest for a debenture of an industrial company!

There are generally several alternative capitalisations possible. Once the right one has been devised and the right price decided upon, the sub-underwriting of the issue, amongst institutions prepared to take up for permanent investment whatever is not subscribed by the public, is comparatively easy. One sub-underwrites an issue by calling on the chairman or managers of the insurance companies, investment trusts and private banks, showing them the draft prospectus, and offering a participation. Their decision may often depend on the reputation of the issuing house and of its directors, as well as on the merit of the investment, as disclosed by the prospectus. I have often found it very exciting doing a selling job on a new issue of several million pounds.

The right price and right capitalisation of an issue means one that is readily acceptable to investors. The right category of investment often means the type fashionable at the time. The 4-per-cent Preference share for G.U.S. already mentioned rose to 21/6d during Mr Dalton's brief period as Chancellor of the Exchequer, when $2\frac{1}{2}$-per-cent Treasury Bonds were quoted at over 100 per cent. The 4-per-cent Preference capital is now covered some sixty times by earnings and assets, but the shares only stand at 12/6d. At the present moment investors are happy in buying certain ordinary shares giving a yield of $1\frac{1}{2}$ per cent to $2\frac{1}{2}$ per cent, though $6\frac{1}{2}$ per cent is the normal rate of interest for gilt-edged securities. The companies are no doubt wise to raise their capital on the cheapest terms possible, but it does not necessarily mean that this will work out well for the investor in future years.

After the disasters following the Wall Street crash of 1930, the American prospectus has been so amended that in its present form it is generally a thirty- or forty-page affair, which, by its details, completely bewilders anyone but a professional investor with long legal training. The American issuing house also has to buy an issue of new shares or debentures outright; it then resells it to institutions and the public. This entails an enormous outlay of capital and heavy expense before the securities reach the individual investor. The British procedure of advertising all the particulars of an issue on one page of a newspaper, gives the investor all the relevant facts and enables him to apply direct for his investment, at a much smaller cost to the company than is the case in the United States. It is the fairest and cheapest way yet devised of issuing new capital on terms which enable the public to participate.

There is a prevalent idea that enormous profits are made in the City by making issues. This is not the case. The average profit for instance, in making an issue of £1,000,000 of Debentures, would be about £5,000 or $\frac{1}{2}$ of 1 per cent.

Against this profit must be set the heavy overhead expenses of the issuing house.

To me, one of the attractions of making issues is the excitement of handling large sums, and continuing to act as financial adviser, and thus being consulted in the development of progressive industrial concerns.

For years I have been able to advise Isaac Wolfson in the set-up of his annual report and chairman's speech, and have had numerous exciting and even amusing moments in being concerned with many of his negotiations for acquiring new businesses, or making new issues on his behalf. The other day I made an issue of Ordinary shares for Mount Royal Limited, on which G.U.S. eventually made the very satisfactory capital profit of £1,800,000. Three days before the issue, however, Isaac Wolfson rang me up from the airport on his way to the South of France, saying that he was concerned at the cost of the printing of the prospectus and thought £100 or so might be saved if the printing were done in one of his own printing works. This shows that despite his having recently donated over £10,000,000 to charity, he still carefully looks after the details of his company's affairs!

My most recent issue before concluding this autobiography was for Charles Forte. The problem was to find £3,000,000 in cash to put into the business and get permission to deal in the company's Ordinary shares (ten votes per share) and Ordinary A shares (one vote per share). As preference shares were not popular at the time the terms were decided, we arranged to make an issue of £1,500,000 7-per-cent Preference shares and 1,500,000 Ordinary shares both at 20/- per share, but no one was to be allowed to apply for Ordinary shares without applying for a similar amount of Preference shares. As it happened it was necessary to issue a further 500,000 Ordinary shares and 400,000 A shares to qualify for a sufficient proportion to get permission to deal in the whole Company's shares and thus save surtax. I therefore undertook that my Ocean Trust should purchase the 500,000 Ordinary shares at 20/6 and the A shares at 20/- and arranged to place them with institutions above that price. The fact that 500,000 Ordinary shares were purchased unconditionally before the issue at 6d above the price paid by the public, was a contributory factor, with Charles Forte's marvellous reputation amongst the millions of customers served in his establishments, in making the issue an outstanding success. The public sent in cash applications for £120 millions, which I believe was a record for any British industrial issue, and the shares soon afterwards rose to 75 per cent above the issue price. I am confident the public will have proved right in their optimism and that over the years the Forte business will parallel Great Universal Stores in growth and development.

There is also a wrong impression about the wealth of leading City professional men. Before making a large issue, I consult a few leading investment managers of insurance companies and chairmen of investment trusts. These men may, as servants of their companies, take a participation of several million pounds, but they are usually men of modest means themselves, looking to their director's fees as a reward for serving the best interests of their shareholders.

I have known chairmen of industrial companies, in the so-called tycoon category, make handsome fortunes by acquiring for their families, or through nominees, blocks of shares of companies, ultimately the subject of take-over bids. But this is quite contrary to the traditions of the City, and in my long experience of amalgamations and negotiations, I have never known a banker or director of an issuing house to take advantage of inside information acquired by advising a client, or through his position as a director of a public company.

When I was banking in New York about thirty years ago, there was a saying that 'a gentleman's agreement lasts as long as the nearest gentleman can reach the nearest telephone'. At any rate one always had to have a lawyer at one's side, and everything countersigned in legal form, before making the slightest commitment. In London I have on occasion signed an underwriting agreement for £2,000,000 or even larger amounts without any more than verbal agreements noted on a piece of paper, for most of the issue. In this small circle we all know and trust each other and every man's word is his bond. Whilst this standard remains, the City will always hold its own.

Making large issues of capital requires a very specialised technique, quite different to that needed for the management of investments where anticipating future long-term economic trends is essential. I have always found the search for capital appreciation a fascinating study; and having entered business with a background of academic training and government service, I have been able to look at some of its problems with some degree of intellectual detachment. Success in this sphere requires a combination of courage and factual knowledge.

Because of my detachment, friends have often sought my advice in these matters. There are many I have tried to save from ruining themselves through over-speculation. Others I have urged to play safe by cashing in paper profits before the tide changed against them. Today, owing to higher taxation and reduced income, many endeavour to obtain a capital profit by changes into more speculative investments; though it may prove speculative to retain gilt-edged securities and conservative to invest in mining shares. I learned from my own youthful experience that, without proper knowledge, it is much easier to lose money than to make it, so that for most people a 'defence policy against loss' is all important.

When I inherited from my father, I found he had a large number of worthless or nearly worthless securities. If some investment turned out wrong he put the security 'in the box', in the hope of it 'coming right some day'. This is what most investors do. They keep their bad investments for ever, whilst taking quick profits on the investments that go up. They are thus apt to make a very large proportional loss on the investments that go wrong, and only a small profit on the winners. This cutting a loss is psychologically a difficult problem. Whenever I am asked to comment on a friend's investment list, I try to sort out, with the best outside advice obtainable, which investments seem promising and reasonable and which appear dubious. I then suggest selling the doubtful ones. This generally meets with the answer that they were bought so much higher, or that this is only a 'paper loss'. Incidentally, the idea of a paper loss is a mental delusion. The market price at which the shares can be sold at that moment is the real loss, the only one that matters. If I then ask, 'Would you buy these doubtful investments at the present price?', the answer is invariably 'No'. The logical sequence is to sell the doubtful shares for whatever cash they will fetch and with that money to buy new investments in companies with good management that are likely to offer scope for rising profits.

The question of cutting a loss is a difficult one. Before the Second World War, London had large investments in the American market. During the Wall Street slump I was so worried by the continual fall of my American shares that I sold them all regardless of loss, and thus, without knowing it at the time, saved a greater loss later. To give an idea of the extent of the fall, I may mention that New York Central, which at that time was considered a safe investment having paid a dividend of $8 a share for years, fell from $240 to $10.

This was a very difficult period for my firm, trying to advise harassed clients what to do about their falling investments. I had a Stock Exchange friend who was a terrific gambler and had lost a fortune. He was going around to all his friends seeking advice. Finally he came to me and told me his position. He had a large number of shares which he had not paid for, which he was carrying on margin, the margin constantly having to be increased with every fall, by selling his investments. Knowing him well, I told him I would not give him any advice unless he allowed me absolute discretion to deal with his position as I thought fit. He refused at first and ran round in a state of shattered nerves asking further advice, trying to find confirmation of his own optimistic views. However, he was soon back in my office, his shares having fallen further, imploring me to do something to help him. I lifted up the telephone, got on to the Stock Exchange and gave an order to sell all his shares. He had not expected me to act so quickly. Wringing his hands he told me I had ruined him, and that he had only £1,800 left in the world. A fortnight later he came back to thank me. If he had kept his position open he would have lost a further £40,000 and been made bankrupt. Today he is a wealthy man again. There was no special merit in my having advised him in this way, as it is one of the laws of nature that it is easier to advise others about how to deal with their problems, than to deal with one's own.

Incidentally, it is a fallacy to think that Stock Exchange members make fortunes by speculation. The contrary is generally the case. I have been told that the Inland Revenue, which has studied their tax-returns over a large number of years, has found that they make money by short-term speculation when markets are rising, but lose a much larger amount when prices fall.

I have usually found that I have had good advice as to what share to buy, but rarely received the same wise counsel as to when to sell. This means that you must generally make your own decision about selling, which entails making a close study of changing industrial trends. In every period there are fashions in investment. The shares in this favoured group eventually go too high and other groups take their place. I remember some time ago the papers only had to mention that a company had an interest in plastic development for the company's shares to rise. A few years ago, companies with an interest in atomic development were, like plastics, considered to have a 'growth' element for the future. These views have been proved wrong owing to overproduction and excessive competition in the plastic field, and the enormous and unproductive capital investment required in atomic development.

Today the fashionable boom is in property shares. There is a sound reason for this, for when rent control was abolished, rents were allowed to soar to famine prices owing to control having hindered normal building for so long; so property values have risen proportionately. This situation may not last for ever. I remember before the war, when I was in New York, Nelson Rockefeller telling me that to find tenants for his grand new office building, he offered them a negligible rental for the first few years, as an inducement to take up long-term leases in the Rockefeller Centre. And history has proved in many countries that property is most vulnerable to Socialist legislation.

Except for someone with very good inside knowledge of a particular company, I would always advise investment in companies with a large capitalisation. There is a free market when shares are rising, and one can sell freely even during a market slump; and if the market leaders are not satisfactory investments, one is not likely to do well in investments in small companies.

The public is often wiser than the City in spotting companies likely to be successful in the future. I once made an issue of £750,000 Preference shares for Macleans Ltd. The company spent over £300,000 a year in advertising, and had only small assets, though the earnings were large and progressive. We only underwrote the issue in the City after considerable difficulty and persuasion. But the issue was enormously over-subscribed by 12,500 applications from the public. They were the ones who had received relief from the famous stomach powders, and knew the value of the business. Years later I negotiated the sale of Macleans to Beecham's for over £3,000,000, and with it went the clever young salesman of Macleans, Mr Lazell, who is now chairman and managing-director of the Beecham's Group. On another occasion we had great difficulty in making a £1,000,000 Debenture issue for Kelly's Directories. We could only get £100,000 underwriting done in London, and only after persuasive meetings with the shrewd Scottish investment trusts in Glasgow, Edinburgh and Dundee, were we able to get the whole issue underwritten for the Camrose and Iliffe group. In fact the issue was enormously over-applied-for by the thousands of users of *The Post Office London Directory*, belonging to Kelly's.

I have often found graphs helpful in considering investment problems. It is not worth making a share graph except of a company with a large capitalisation and a free market. A graph shows you in a pictorial form how the share has acted in the past, i.e., how its shareholders (large and small) have determined its movements. This forms a helpful guide for the future. The theory is that a share graph indicates changes of policy by the board of directors or changes in the fortunes of the company, often more clearly than if one had inside information. I have been intimately concerned with industrial negotiations of considerable magnitude; and I have often noticed that the share graph gave a better indication as to whether or not a deal would go through than I could give myself, familiar with every phase of the negotiation.

I believe such graphs can be really helpful to the student of market conditions, provided he can learn to interpret what the graph has to say, which is the most difficult problem. I do not believe they can be of much assistance in spotting short-term trends, but can on occasion indicate an opportunity to sell an existing investment or to purchase a share where the possibility of profit seems exceptional. It may also confirm or refute a view derived from a careful statistical survey of the company's prospects.

One very interesting element in investment is to try and spot a long-term change of trend, indicating when you should sell out or when you should purchase a share with the possibility of large capital appreciation. The game requires a great deal of patience and timing is all important. A share is not cheap because it has fallen to half its former level nor dear because it has risen to twice the price of the original investment.

I have often found graphs the best way of spotting this change of trend. Ever since I worked in America in my early youth, I have been fascinated by the study of share graphs, and have generally had graphs made of the leading shares I am interested in, showing the weekly high and low over a period of years.

The most interesting signal a graph can give is if, after a long period of falling prices, it moves sideways for some time within a narrow margin. When it at last moves upwards out of this narrow range, it gives an indication of a long-term upward trend. In the same way, if the graph of a share shows that prices have fluctuated within a certain range for a number of years, and that range has been broken on the downward side, it would indicate that some new unfavourable factor has occurred. It would be foolish to suggest that the study of share graphs takes the place of a prudent and constructive investment policy, but it can be a valuable adjunct.

It also clearly illustrates the principle that if you make a speculative investment, it is wise in buying to decide the level at which to cut your loss if you are mistaken; and never to average. On the contrary, instead of averaging when you are wrong, it is better to buy further shares at rising prices when you are right. Thus your investment is increased if you spot a real winner, and you have limited losses when you have backed the wrong horse.

In industry it may also prove helpful to spot important changes in the trend of the commodities one deals with. As chairman of Jeremiah Ambler Ltd and other woollen textile companies, I was especially worried in the early fifties by the continuous rise in the price of raw wool to record prices, touching as high as 320/- a lb. The graph did not help, as it continued to show new high prices being reached and hardly any reaction. One needed the wool to maintain current orders, and keep men in full employment, but any substantial fall might have led to enormous stock losses. Timing was all important.

The first danger signal occurred when my co-director, Sir Colin Gubbins, told me he had just returned from a holiday in Cyprus, where the local population were selling the wool from their old mattresses and getting something like one pound sterling for every one lb. of wool. It recalled the occasion before the war when a few speculators thought they could corner the world-market in pepper, only to discover that the high price brought out large hidden reserves from the Middle and Far East. It was a danger signal but not quite enough to make me take the plunge.

Then one day, out of the blue, *The Times* published a leading article about wool, saying that its record price was nevertheless justified for a number of reasons. This rang a bell. *The Times* nearly always confines such topics to its City page. To bring them under the heading of current topics reminded me of the headlines in the American press just before the Wall Street crash, and the old saying, 'Sell when the world is full of hope; buy when your nerves are frayed'. I at once gave orders for Jeremiah Ambler to sell the whole of its large stock of wool at the best price obtainable, despite considerable resistance from the technical staff. Wool is now standing at a third of its former price. This shows that academic and economic training can, at times, prove helpful in solving business problems.

Chapter Twelve

★

MARRIAGE AND FRIENDSHIPS

ONE DAY towards the end of the war, I was going up in the lift to my flat at 55 Park Lane, when I noticed a particularly pretty young woman. Being my usual romantic self, I began to talk to her and found she was going to tea with a mutual friend, who lived above me. She turned out to be Princess Irina Obolensky, whose brother Alex I had met several times at parties. I fell very much in love with her, and in fact, we were married three weeks later.

By an extraordinary coincidence she was living in a house in Bruton Street, where Colin Gubbins and I had shared a flat earlier in the war. We had left it because the building had been badly shaken by bombs. I persuaded her to move at once to a concrete-built hotel, and thereby probably saved her life, for the ceiling and walls of her former room collapsed during an air-raid a few days later.

When next I met our mutual friend, she jokingly said that she had warned Irina against me. I got quite a kick out of answering that Irina had obviously taken no notice of her advice, since our wedding was to take place the following week.

The ceremony was performed in the Russian Orthodox Church, our two sponsors, Prince Galitzine and my old friend Sir Frank Newnes, precariously suspending crowns over our heads, to the accompaniment of a powerful Russian choir with deep bass voices.

Being then without parents or brothers or sisters, I looked forward with pleasure to entering a ready-made family, but I soon discovered that Russian family life and outlook were strangely different to our own.

My father-in-law, Prince Serge Obolensky, a direct descendant of King Harold of 1066 fame, was a small, shy man with very charming manners, and I took an immediate liking to him. His wife, Luba, a dark, active little woman, whose old photographs showed her to have been very beautiful, was, however, the mainstay of the family. It was she who had had the burden of bringing up six children with the help of their aged Russian nanny. It was she who always found suitable lodgers for the empty rooms in their rambling house in Muswell Hill, originally given to them by a generous old man called Mr Frank Green, whom Princess Marie-Louise had asked to help the family when they first arrived from Moscow. In fact I discovered that Mr Green had kept the whole family for the last twenty-five years, and paid for all the children's schooling, and for the oldest son's education at Oxford. I never met Mr Green, and by the time I came into the family his benefactions to them had diminished, since he was then over eighty and had been hit financially by the war.

It was difficult for me to get used to the haphazard *nitchevo* way of life in the Obolensky family. I remember admiring the garden of their house at Muswell Hill which, though neglected, was full of blossom in the early spring. 'Oh, we never go into it any more,' they explained; 'The iron steps leading down from the sitting room were broken a long time ago.'

As I saw that my father-in-law was always sitting in a corner at home doing crossword puzzles and saying he had nothing to interest him any longer, I tried several times to find him some easy, congenial occupation, or to associate him with some of my political activities. He was most appreciative of my efforts, but nothing really seemed to rouse

L

him. I was, however, able to bring one enjoyment back into his life, by arranging for him to go to Paris once a year to attend the dinner of the Chevaliers Gardes (corresponding to our Horse Guards) where an ever-diminishing number of brother officers would meet and talk over the 'good old days'. He often spoke to me about the dinners, and he made me realise the personal tragedy of these old men who had started life in carefree fashion, and now in foreign lands were so ill-equipped to face their personal problems.

Not long after my marriage, I had a telephone call from Abinger one August day to say the nearby church had been hit by a V-bomb and the house badly damaged by blast, but that Violet and Sydney and the household were safe.

An hour later I arrived in Abinger to find the entire village on the scene. I rushed over to Violet, who was lying on a mattress on the lawn. She told me her bedroom door had been blown over her bed by the blast, injuring her back, but that after a couple of aspirins she was not in pain. She appeared serene and in good spirits as she always was in an emergency. Max Beerbohm and his wife Florence were standing beside her. Their cottage had fortunately escaped damage.

Much of the roof of the manor was down, most of the windows broken and all the inside of the house covered with plaster from the old-fashioned lath and plaster ceilings. I found Sydney in the house with Violet's old maid Cameron, desperately searching for a clean suit and a silk shirt from a cupboard, in a room covered with dust and debris. Although he appeared very shaken, he insisted on being elegantly dressed as usual, and was fussily selecting the right tie to go with his pale grey flannels.

Fortunately I was able to secure rooms for them at the Sackville Hotel in Hove, where they had often stayed before. Presently an ambulance arrived to fetch them, and I followed with the rest of the household in my car.

It was a touching send-off on that beautiful summer

morning. I could not help noticing with sorrow how cruelly the flowering shrubs and roses, then at their best, and each one chosen with loving care by Sydney, contrasted with the ruins around. Abinger friends, old and young, were saying goodbye to Violet and Sydney, and dear old Max, while trying to joke, had tears in his eyes as they drove away.

Once in Hove, Violet remained in bed for three weeks, but she suffered from the pain of her fractured spine for the rest of her life. Sydney, who was seventy-six and in delicate health, had put on a brave front when the disaster occurred, but he suddenly collapsed and died two months later from delayed shock. Up to the last day he had been rereading *Talks with Tolstoi* and short stories by Thomas Mann.

I was terribly concerned about how Violet, then nearing seventy, would stand up to this dreadful blow. But not for one moment did she involve others in her heartbreak and sorrow. Courageously and resolutely she set about remaking her life. After the war she returned to her London home and gradually picked up the threads of her former existence. She continued to educate the twelve-year-old refugee girl she had adopted during the war. She went on giving me singing lessons. As in the past, she remained the sympathetic counsellor of her younger friends. She arranged for Sydney's long novel *A True Story* to be reprinted, incorporating many revisions he had desired. Unfortunately this reissue was done by Peter Baker's new publishing firm, The Falcon Press, which shortly afterwards went into liquidation as he was sent to prison. The new edition was dispersed and the book is still unavailable.

Over the next ten years Violet translated some famous French novels, such as *Le Bal du Comte d'Orgel* by Raymond Radiguet, *Marie Donadieu*, by Charles-Louis Philippe, and among contemporary novels, *Julietta*, by Louise de Vilmorin.

Though she hardly ever went out, friends were constantly with her, and new ones sought the privilege of knowing her, including authors writing the lives of Caruso, Puccini, Paolo

WORKING MEN'S COLLEGE

Tosti and Oscar Wilde, who came to her for first-hand information and advice.

Hardly a day passed when I was in London without a long telephone-call from her, or my dropping in to see her. Gradually we began to talk about Sydney together, recalling various incidents and remarking how pleased he would have been to know of this or that event in my life or in the lives of others he had known. So we were able to talk of him not only as a happy memory, cherished and shared, but still an influence in my daily life.

Until she was eighty-six, Violet's mind was as alert and active as ever. Then she had a stroke and became seriously ill. But before this she often told me what a marvellous life she had had, and how pleased Sydney would have been to know that his dying wish had been fulfilled by the loving care I had taken of her.

Mrs Freda Gardner, who had been Sydney's secretary, was Violet's devoted companion to the very end.

After Violet's recent death, T. S. Eliot wrote this lovely tribute in *The Times*:

'I write not only to express a personal sorrow but because of my memories of Violet and her husband, the late Sydney Schiff, in the world of art and letters forty years ago. In the 1920's the Schiffs' hospitality, generosity, and encouragement meant much to a number of young artists and writers of whom I was one. The Schiffs' acquaintance was cosmopolitan, and their interests embraced all the arts. At their house I met, for example, Delius and Arthur Symons, and the first Viscountess Rothermere, who founded *The Criterion* under my editorship. Middleton Murry and Katherine Mansfield knew their house, and Wyndham Lewis and Charles Scott-Moncrieff, and many others.

'When I married in 1957, Violet welcomed me and my wife, whom she took to her heart at once. She was already an invalid and could not be persuaded to pay visits, but was always happy to receive her friends. Her mind was as active as ever, and her interest in people and in the arts was undiminished. It was, indeed, in her last years when she was house-bound and, I suspect, often in pain, that her qualities impressed me most deeply: the vigour of her speech, the animation of her face, and the warmth of her sympathy. Hers was a sympathy which made one feel that she understood much more than had been, or could be, put into words; that she was aware of, and responded to, that which could not be spoken. In consequence of this sensitiveness she could regard people with a gentle, clear-sighted charity.

'I write primarily to pay homage to a beloved friend, but also in the hope that some future chronicler of the history of art and letters in our time may give to Sydney and Violet Schiff the place which is their due.'

At the end of the war I again met Prince Paul of Yugoslavia, my old friend from Oxford days, whom I discovered knew many of my wife's family, and whom I had not seen during the war years. But I must now return to the summer before the war to explain the circumstances through which this friendship was renewed.

In July 1938, I went to stay with Bojo Banac, at his seaside home near Dubrovnik. It was a gay house-party which included besides Madame Banac's own family, Natasha Bagration, Mary Cunningham-Reid, and a continuous stream of new friends.

From this vantage point I was able to observe and learn something of Yugoslav peasant life. On Sundays the women wore their beautiful native dresses for church, with various distinguishing coloured ribbons in their head-dress to show whether they were married, engaged or single. The men occupied the pews on the right and the women those on the left. Market days reflected the primitive nature of their agriculture, since from first light one saw whole families on the roads dragging or carrying their produce to the local market, which might be as much as three or four hours away.

I also had the opportunity of seeing some of the works of

the great contemporary Yugoslav sculptor, Mestrovic, who had designed a fine memorial chapel built by Banac in memory of his first wife. Epstein is the only English sculptor I would compare with Mestrovic, as they both did splendid bronze statues, but I consider Mestrovic to have been the finer artist, as he was equally skilled in the delicate carving of marble.

Banac had one of the biggest yachts in the Mediterranean, and we all went for a cruise along the Dalmatian coast, the party including the Duke and Duchess of Kent, who were able to escape from the round of public duties and have a really relaxed holiday. As we approached Split we saw the great Mestrovic monument near the harbour, which stands sixty feet high against a background of Roman ruins, and represents a priest who was a national hero. It is the most imposing statue I have ever seen.

On my way home I thought I would pay a visit to my old friend, Prince Paul. I remembered him as a charming and sympathetic man, who had a great love of art and like his friend, Kenneth Clark, had studied with Bernhard Berenson, the well-known authority on Italian painting. Prince Paul had very close ties with our Royal Family, and life in England made a great appeal to him. So he had chosen to stay here after leaving Oxford. I could have imagined him as a don or perhaps a director of a national art gallery. However, after the assassination of his cousin, King Alexander, he returned to Yugoslavia to act as regent to the young King Peter, his strong sense of duty having prevailed over his personal inclinations.

When I visited him he had been in charge of his country's affairs for four years. Driving towards his residence in Brdo, I wondered if I should find him very changed. The way was difficult to find, but soon an ever-increasing number of soldiers on the road was a clear indication that I was getting closer. The place itself was rather like a large English country house except that it was heavily guarded. Plainclothes men even patrolled the lawn, where I found Princess Olga and her father, Prince Nicholas of Greece, sitting peacefully under a tree, whilst the children played nearby under the watchful eyes of their English nanny.

Prince Paul began by showing me his fine collection of modern paintings, including those of Yugoslav painters. He spoke of some of his worries, of the inefficiency of the bureaucracy, about the backwardness of the country and the conflicting groups in Yugoslav politics, telling me of the uphill battle he was fighting in trying to introduce necessary reforms. Later we all had tea on the lawn. The shadows were growing long when I took my leave, sadly reflecting that he was obviously too civilised and cultured a man to be able to enforce his enlightened views upon his country. I felt he was up against great difficulties which he would have to face alone and unaided.

It was not until many years later that I met him again, as an exile from his country. The story of Prince Paul's role in the last war was never rightly presented in Britain. Two books which have recently been published throw quite a new light on his activities as Prince Regent: these are the *British Official History of the Second World War*, and *Yugoslavia in Crisis, 1934–1941*, published by the Columbia University Press. Our official history states that 'Prince Paul himself seemed to be sincere in wishing for a British victory, but his military advisers told him that Yugoslavia could not hold out for more than a week against the Germans, and that, even with British help, the Greeks could not resist much longer.'[1] Threatened by a possible German invasion when there were no Allies to help him, he tried to temporise to avoid an open break. His government, after continuous pressure, finally signed the Tripartite Pact under conditions 'that obliged the Axis powers to respect the integrity and sovereignty of Yugoslavia and not to ask Yugoslavia for permission to move military forces across her territory in

[1] *British Foreign Policy in the Second World War*, p. 137.

time of war'.[1] These were the best terms obtainable, and the last condition was more than even neutral Sweden had been able to get, for she had 'signed an agreement with Germany permitting a steady flow of traffic to pass over her border'.[2] Prince Paul hoped by this means that his country could remain independent for another year or so until the Allies were sufficiently strong for Yugoslav intervention on their side to be effective. But at this crucial moment, Simovic, an ambitious general with little political wisdom, organised a revolution to depose Prince Paul, hoaxing the population into supporting him by a voice on the radio purporting to be King Peter's.[3]

However, General Simovic, when he took office, had to face the same problem as Prince Paul. 'He therefore continued the regency policy of neutrality and adherence to the Tripartite Pact.'[4] Our official history states that 'General Simovic told Mr Campbell (the British ambassador) that his policy towards Germany was to gain time, and that he did not want us to force him into any move likely to provoke Hitler'. Like Prince Paul 'he did not want Mr Eden to come to Belgrade' and 'had accepted an Italian offer of mediation'. 'General Simovic said that the new Yugoslav Foreign Minister might go to Germany.' 'The Germans did not allow General Simovic the time he had hoped to gain.'[5] On 6 April, one week after the Simovic revolution, they attacked Yugoslavia and Greece. The Greek army, despite a heroic resistance and the help of British forces, was soon forced to capitulate.

The Yugoslav army, unable fully to mobilise in time, and without material or military help from Britain, was destroyed within a few days. Nearly a million Yugoslavs were killed in the war and the civil strife that followed, and the country was ultimately delivered to Communist rule.

---

[1] *Yugoslavia in Crisis, 1934–1941*, Columbia University Press, 1962, p. 240.   [2] *Ibid.*, p. 299.   [3] *Ibid.*, p. 262.   [4] *Ibid.*, p. 297. [5] *British Foreign Policy in the Second World War*, p. 138.

Revelations from the German archives, discovered after the war, also prove that Prince Paul acted in quite a different light from that put forward by the British newspapers at the time and had all along defended the Allied cause. Even our own official history now reveals that he gave advance warning to Britain that Hitler had told him that Germany would attack Russia on 30 June 1941. He obviously tried his utmost to save his people from disaster. As for the heroic General Simovic, he soon abandoned his army and took refuge in England, where I met him safely settled in a cottage in the country.

As a result of the Simovic revolution Prince Paul had asked the British government if he might retire to one of the British colonies. This request was readily granted and he went to Kenya, and later to South Africa.

Flying over to Johannesburg on a business trip after the war, I telephoned him in the hope of seeing him again. It was a very saddened man who dined with me in my hotel sitting-room. I felt deeply moved by his unhappy situation and longed to do anything possible to help him. After the first long exchange of confidences he noticed a piano with music on it, and suggested we should try some songs. He was an excellent pianist and, what is more, a most understanding accompanist, and I sang with him until the early hours of the morning. The songs of Fauré, Renaldo Hahn and Ravel revived memories of his early youth and the cultured atmosphere he had missed in wartime Johannesburg. Singing that night to the accompaniment of an old upright piano thousands of miles from home was a happy experience for us both and helped to cement our old friendship.

The next time I saw Prince Paul was when Irina and I met him at Geneva on his return from South Africa. As he left the aeroplane and came towards us with a happy smile on his face, I realised what a significant moment this must be for him. After six years exiled in Africa he was not only returning to Europe and civilisation, but to Geneva, where he had spent much of his boyhood, and where he felt specially at home. His high spirits were infectious, and after a sumptuous lunch at the Mère Royaume, we set out on a nostalgic pilgrimage. We wandered about the streets while he recalled pleasant memories. His delight at finding much unchanged and his happiness at being in Europe again, made this an enchanted day for all three of us, and one I shall never forget.

Prince Paul had always been a great admirer of Proust and one day I happened to mention that only a short time before I had again come across the old Comtesse Greffuhle, then over ninety, who was supposed to have been the model for the Duchesse de Guermantes in *À la Recherche du Temps Perdu*. She had been staying at the same hotel as I had in Geneva and we had lunched together. Madame Greffuhle had been an old friend of Father's, but I had not seen her since his death.

However, I soon discovered that despite her great age, she still retained her former enthusiasm for trying to get others to support any idea she was keen about. I well remember Father and myself staying a weekend at her wonderful château at Bois Boudran, and her gaily forcing her guests, including a very reluctant British ambassador and the head of the Quai d'Orsay, to play charades. She was a woman of great vitality with remarkable social gifts, and she had really believed she was playing a big part in politics, at a time when there was much controversy in Franco-British relations, by making these two old men join in parlour games together. In the same way she had now taken up yoga, and in Geneva had given me a number of pamphlets which she assured me would change my life, whilst she begged me to come and see her again when next I was in Paris.

Prince Paul had never met her, and so I arranged that we would call on her together. Before our visit, I went to the florist opposite the Ritz, to send Madame Greffuhle some flowers. The old lady who took the order was surprised that 'cette chère Madame' was still alive, as she had not sent flowers there for years. She told me how, as a young girl, she had enjoyed helping to arrange the floral decorations for the very grand receptions at her house.

It was with pleasurable anticipation that we arrived, with Princess Olga, at 8 Rue d'Astorg. The entrance was through an enormous black carriage-door in the middle of a high, stone wall. I seemed to be following in the footsteps of one of the characters in *Du Côté de Chez Swann* as I crossed the big courtyard towards the shadowy house of the 'Duchesse de Guermantes' beyond!

When I had been there twenty-five years before, footmen in livery had opened the door, and I remembered the beautiful eighteenth-century interior, the Aubusson carpets, the magnificent chandeliers, the lovely pictures, and the exquisite taste with which every room was furnished. Now the door was opened by a very old man in shabby clothes, who silently led us through a deserted hall, up dusty, uncarpeted stairs, past cold, empty salons, with large white spaces where pictures had formerly hung. We followed him up and up until we came to a long narrow staircase leading to the fifth floor which must formerly have been the servants' quarters. There, at the very top of the house, in a very small room, we found Madame Greffuhle and her younger sister, the Princesse de Caraman-Chimay. Madame Greffuhle, still tall and thin, with bright vivacious eyes, had obviously taken great pains over her appearance. She wore a black silk scarf wound like a turban round her hair. Her neck was swathed in white net, and long white gloves came up above her elbows. She had on a black silk dress but no jewels, and had somehow contrived an impression of unusual elegance. Her sister was plump and comfortable-looking.

It was winter, and the little room was heated by an old-fashioned black stove. Madame Greffuhle made no excuses for receiving us in what seemed a deserted house, and gave no explanation of the changes of fortune that had occasioned it. On the contrary, she asked us if we had seen the famous statue of Diane the Huntress by Houdon in the hall, the only work of art I had noticed in the building. She told us a long story about how it had been bequeathed to her by an admirer whom she had only met once in her life.

Talking of Proust, she called him 'le petit Marcel', and said she had sometimes been helpful in giving him the names of 'de grandes couturières' for his girl-friends; she seemed surprised that he had become so famous and so much talked about. When referring to my father and mother, or to Marcel Proust, she mentioned incidents which must have happened half a century before, as if they had occurred yesterday. After a further exchange of courtesies we took our departure, still amazed by the quiet, unhurried ease with which she and her devoted sister had received us in their attic, just as if they had been sitting in her grand drawing-room of former days.

Prince Paul now lives in Paris and Florence, and we meet as often as circumstances allow. Perhaps of all my friends he is the one whose tastes are most similar to my own. So we can talk freely on a great variety of subjects, for he has an intimate understanding of politics and investments as well as being a connoisseur of the arts. When we visit a picture gallery together, it is inevitable that our gaze will alight on the same pictures and our preferences coincide. Quite apart from his inborn kindness and his remarkable culture, the quality I find most delightful of all is his youthful capacity for enjoying the moment, despite the tragic circumstances in his life.

Another of my old friends whom I met again after the war was Charlie Chaplin, who came to London with his lovely young wife Oona. He was then a very worried man and wanted to leave America and settle in Europe. I saw him as the little Charlie of his films, surrounded by a hostile world! I helped him with the arrangements for making his new film, *The King in New York*, in England; and discussing different possibilities, finally suggested he should take up residence near the Lake of Geneva. We went to Lausanne together, enquired of a local agent about houses, and he fell in love with, and bought, the first house we visited on the hills above Vevey, which is now his home.

I have never discussed politics with Charlie, as I have always found artists naïve and misinformed about such matters, even if some of them think their views of importance. I have heard it said that Charlie is a Communist, though to my knowledge nobody could be more capitalistic-minded, or more vigilant over his investments and expenditure. He has an immense fortune, but has told me that the poverty of his early youth is so vivid that one of his greatest fears is that this will happen to him again.

Shortly after he had transferred his assets to Switzerland he rang me up begging me to come and see him to discuss a most serious matter. Meeting me for lunch at the Savoy Grill, he seemed so agitated and nervous, that I myself became apprehensive and begged him to tell me all his troubles before we looked at the menu and ordered lunch. He mentioned a bank I had recommended to him, where he had an account, and said he was terribly worried as to whether the money was safe there. I asked him what was the sum involved and he said it was about $2,000,000. I could not help laughing as I told him that I certainly would not have any worries myself, if I were lucky enough to have such a large fortune on current account at one of the largest joint-stock banks in Switzerland! But that is Charlie.

The delight of his company stems from the exuberance of his personality. Immediately after our lunch at the Savoy he took me to Pinewood Studios where he was directing the musical part of his film. To my amazement he was in entire command of the orchestral and musical direction just as if he had been a trained musician. He can only play in one key, but I have sat up all night with him while he improvised new tunes on the piano. I have often been enchanted at his original and natural musical talent, which has made him a popular song writer, whose tunes circle the world. Apart from *Monsieur Verdoux*, the story in most of his films is partly autobiographical, being related to some aspect of his own life, as with the great novels of Tolstoi, and Marcel Proust. *The King in New York* referred to the problems of his leaving the United States. *Limelight* is a story of a man of his age marrying someone like Oona, so very much younger than himself. In *The Circus* one sees the little man, who would like to play the role of the hero to the girl he loves, but is finally left sad and alone in the world, a theme that occurs in so many of his films and so often in his life.

I am certain that many of Charlie's films will be seen again by future generations, as today we read the books of gifted writers of the past.

One day in London he told me how worried he was that his children should be living with him at the Savoy, as hotel life was so bad for children. However, at last his worries were over. The children's English nanny, whom he had brought back from America, knew of a lovely inn in the country near the town where she was born, and he had arranged to send them all there.

Charlie is a marvellous mimic and when he describes something he conjures up the imagery of a motion picture. He described the English countryside where the children would be living; white clouds floating across a blue sky, the cows with cool wet noses browsing in the green meadows. I asked him where this idyllic inn was situated. 'A place called Coventry', he replied. I thought of the engineering factory in Coventry of which I was chairman, employing some 15,000 workers. I had never seen any cows browsing in green meadows there. I explained to Charlie that Coventry was the English counterpart of Detroit. 'Oh, my poor children,' he said with tears in his eyes. Once again I was moved by his distress, and impulsively invited the whole family to stay with me in the country for a week or so whilst he and Oona looked for something suitable. Oona, Charlie, two nannies and four children arrived the next day.

Charlie was enchanted with the Surrey countryside, the old church, the stocks on the village green, and my Guernsey cows. A day or so later he and Oona kissed the children goodbye, and that was the last we saw or heard of them for some months. We immediately had to get two extra staff; the weather turned cold and I bought them all some warm clothes. The children were accustomed to getting up at eleven and going to bed twelve hours later, which bewildered my little son Serge, brought up in English fashion by a very strict nanny; but they were adorable and everyone loved them. The Chaplins had completely disappeared, leaving no address. It was an unusual situation. One day out of the blue came a telegram from Charlie asking me to dispatch the children at once to Geneva, where he would meet them. As I kissed their trusting little faces goodbye, I knew I would always miss them.

The next time Charlie came to England he never even rang me up, though I had left numerous messages for him at the Savoy. At the time I was very hurt, for I was experiencing once again what has so often happened to me before; the realisation that my judgment has been proved wrong and that my friends fall below my expectations.

No doubt if I had turned up at his hotel he would have enjoyed seeing me, but he was just incapable of making the effort to telephone or of taking any initiative, being too busy with his own affairs at that moment.

As it is not in my nature to be angry for long, I soon put this incident out of my mind, and when we meet, which we do quite often, I enjoy his delightful company as much as ever, and the pleasure of seeing Oona and the children again.

As Charlie was living so near I arranged for him to meet my friend Oskar Kokoschka, who lived in Territet. The meeting was not very successful, as Charlie was in a very self-centred mood, and only wanted to talk about himself, and Oskar, in the midst of painting large scenery-designs for an opera to be performed at Salzburg, only wanted to talk about his pictures. But before they met I told Charlie something of Oskar's life and the unusual circumstances of our first meeting.

It happened this way. In the latter part of the war I gave an informal cocktail party in my small flat, which soon became overcrowded, as many of my guests had brought friends. Moving to greet them I heard an unknown voice talking to a group around a photograph[1] coloured on ivory of a girl of eighteen, dressed in the fashion of the late-Victorian era. 'What a lovely face. A girl with such a warm, generous nature, and those deep, limpid eyes must have suffered greatly in her life! One never meets women like that nowadays in this harsh world!' This was my introduction to Oskar Kokoschka, who had been brought to the party by my friend Chatin Sarachi. How could one fail to be drawn to someone talking about one's own mother in a manner I later learned was so characteristic of his sensitive and attractive personality.

Before the war he had been one of the best-known painters in Central Europe, and also had a well-deserved reputation as a writer of plays and short stories. He had emigrated to England and abandoned all his possessions in Vienna, preferring freedom to living in Austria under Hitler. Though famous in his own country, little notice was taken of him in wartime Britain, and he lived in reduced circumstances on the occasional pictures he was able to sell to the few who recognised the unique genius of his painting.

Soon we became the closest of friends. What attracted me especially was the simple, innate goodness of the man and his exuberant generosity. His wife, Olda, was obliged to look after his money, as he was apt to empty his pockets and give their contents to any poor person he met in the street. There are, indeed, numerous instances of his complete

[1] See the illustration facing page 4.

The Matterhorn, by Oskar Kokoschka

My guide, William Perren, by Stanley Spencer

selflessness. In 1943 he had painted a most powerful portrait of M. Maisky, the Soviet ambassador. He told me his idea was to sell it and give the proceeds to the Stalingrad Fund to be distributed 'to the victims of both sides' (he has always preached forgiveness). The picture itself he wanted the purchaser to present to the Moscow Art Gallery.

The problem was to find a generous donor. I finally persuaded Mr Dreyfus, the chairman of The British Celanese Company and well-known for his philanthropy, to donate £1,000 for the purchase of the picture. It was characteristic of Oskar Kokoschka, who probably did not have £200 in the world at the time, to give £1,000 for a charitable purpose. This sum was more than twice the price of any picture sold by Kokoschka since he had left Vienna.

A strange set of circumstances arose over Maisky's portrait. I had been discussing with Anthony Eden the possibility of the presentation of this picture as a small token of Anglo-Russian goodwill, when I was asked urgently to call on Mr Maisky, who had just returned from Russia. I arrived at the Soviet Embassy in Kensington Park Gardens and rang the bell. As I waited outside, a little peephole in the door was opened, from which I saw two eyes peering at me. When at last I was admitted to the Embassy I was followed into the waiting-room by two men, who remained there but did not speak a word to me. Finally, I was shown into the ambassador's room, where I also found Madame Maisky. To my astonishment, the first thing Mr Maisky did was to take the precaution of locking the three doors leading into the room. Then he asked me not to press for the picture by Kokoschka to be sent to the Moscow Art Gallery since, owing to wartime conditions, 'it would never arrive there safely'. He also asked me to omit any mention of the proposed gift of the portrait in any official communications to the Embassy concerning the generous donation of the money. His wife begged me to do as he wished, and I suddenly realised that Maisky was probably a victim of one of Stalin's ruthless purges. Both of them appeared to be very nervous, and I was quite moved by Madame Maisky's obvious devoted love for her husband, and her anxiety to shield him in any way that lay in her power.

I have often wondered what happened to Maisky back in Russia. He made many friends in Britain, and I heard from one of them who had been to call on him whilst on a goodwill mission to Moscow about ten years ago, that Maisky had opened the door of his small flat but refused to let him in, whispering in urgent tones, 'You will only endanger me if you try to see me'. As for the Maisky portrait, when Russia refused to accept it, I arranged for it to be donated to the Tate Gallery, where it now hangs.

When we first met during the war, Oskar was living in a tiny flat in a rickety old building in St John's Wood, using the little sitting-room as his studio. Because of the bombing I insisted on getting him a flat in a concrete building and furnished it for him and also lent him a studio at the top of my offices in Park Lane, which had a good north light. There are times in life when it is an absolute duty to oneself to help people like Oskar; but it was not easy to make him accept. He once wrote me, in his funny English, 'If I go on becoming indebted to you like this I see in the future a general vague conviction implanted in you that you will finally feel a grievance as if I were careless in our mutual friendship and all the benefit would lay on my side.' But eventually I made him feel that I was only doing in a small way what he would have done if the circumstances had been reversed. I was very happy when he finally assented. He wrote me, 'You bring back to me a time when I was like you are today and when I acted as you do and shared your aspirations and what you are; initiated by love, you represent today in the fireless cheerless house we call our world, the spark of triumphant imagination.' It was much too generous on his part.

Oskar was deeply distressed when his beloved Austria, which had suffered under the tyranny of Hitler and the destruction of war, was finally occupied by Soviet troops. But his underlying faith never deserted him. 'To be loyal to the past and from that source to draw the inspiration and strength to endure the present, that seems to me the only reasonable attitude for someone like me. I have to face life as it is, with all the misery and destruction.' Writing at the time about *Peer Gynt*, the play by Ibsen we saw in London, he said: 'It is a masterful performance. There is no need to enlarge on the greatness of the play, which belongs to the few classical works created since the Greeks first kindled the torch. The unique message of the play, where it differs from all literature, is that man must love, because he dies if he is alone. This is the greatest wisdom, the only one necessary to know, and a wisdom totally forgotten by the warring governments, which order their people to destroy each other. The unique truth is: Love!! Because of his Peer Gynt, Ibsen is to me the greatest poet, for he tells men that it is not the struggle for survival, nor food nor clothes and houses, nor the great power of Hate — but only the supreme realisation of love that makes "the dead awaken".'

After the armistice was proclaimed, Kokoschka told me he kept thinking of what would happen to the poor children in Vienna and other towns in the defeated countries, and feared many would suffer starvation as they did after the First World War. Pondering over these sombre thoughts, he had made a large poster[1] in charcoal of Christ bending down from the Cross and blessing some children. Above the Cross were the words, 'In memory of the children of Europe who have to die of cold and hunger this Xmas'. He lamented that he could only express his fear and anguish in artistic form. But fortunately I was able to give practical effect to his feelings of compassion.

With the help of my friend, John Metcalf, I had over a thousand copies of the poster put up on the London buses and Underground stations for a month before Christmas. It

[1] See the illustration facing page 168.

was done anonymously, with only the unknown signature of O. Kokoschka on this very beautiful picture. Our hope was that, among the millions of people who saw it, some would be reminded, if only for a moment, of the innocent victims of the war.

However hard up he was at times, Kokoschka never once considered lowering his artistic standards for commercial considerations. He refused to have a dealer to sell his pictures, as he did not wish to be pressed to produce more than he felt was artistically desirable. So many French artists of real talent have been undermined by being forced by dealers, and their growing personal demands for money, to paint more and more pictures, which gradually become copies of past efforts: and thus destroyed the dedicated sustained effort needed for artistic creation. Kokoschka is a beautiful water-colourist, and paints flowers in the tradition of the Chinese, but in the more difficult technique of colour instead of black and white. In this, as in all his other work, he is only satisfied with perfection, and I have seen him tear up many beautiful water-colours on which he has spent hours and hours because of some imagined flaw.

He once told me, 'I cannot do my work quickly. It has to mature like the fruits of the earth.' When he starts a picture he never knows how long it will take or whether it will satisfy him, so he may go on painting it for a year or more. When I first met him I wanted to buy one of his pictures, but he had nothing for sale as he was working on several canvasses and did not know when they would be finished. Finally I bought *The Crab* from a lady who had perhaps been over-persuaded by Sarachi to buy it and was pleased to find someone to take it off her hands. From the point of view of painting technique, this is perhaps one of his finest pictures. It represents an enormous crab, with the cliffs of Polperro in Cornwall in the background. In the sea is a small figure trying to swim. Kokoschka said the swimmer was himself, and represents poor Czechoslovakia. The crab

Oskar Kokoschka's poster for the tramways and Underground

Threnody, by Oskar Kokoschka

represents Mr Neville Chamberlain, who would only have to put out one claw to save him from drowning, but remains aloof. The painting of the sea and cliffs has been done by layers of paint being superimposed at different periods. This now gives a great sense of depth like a piece of sculpture. If one isolates any one inch of the picture, one finds it is composed of innumerable colours. And above all, the picture illustrates Kokoschka's main thesis in painting: to display the immense distance that exists between the foreground and the horizon.

At our first meeting Kokoschka had asked to borrow my mother's picture, as he wanted to study it quietly and 'look into her eyes'. A year later he showed me a picture he had painted with the thought of her in mind. I greatly treasure it today. He called it 'Threnody, a great word, meaning a lament sung in memory of somebody who is no longer with us. The Greeks didn't say we go nowhere. Only that we go away. And that is eminently human.'

After the war he wrote me from Zermatt, describing his original conception of the view I love best in the world and which he knew would delight me. 'I have just finished your picture of the Matterhorn,[1] from the Riffelalp Hotel, from which I faced this phenomenon. You will own a wilderness of light and amorphous crags, rocks, solid earth-crust, contrasting with each other. You can wander in this alpine world without risking a broken ankle, embracing nature, undisturbed by human shortcomings like factories, benzine tanks: in short, technical civilisation. Look at the depth of composition which forces you to choose your point of view amid the immense space, otherwise you will be left outside the world created by colour and emotion.'

Kokoschka is also a great portrait-painter, of which the Maisky portrait is a fine example. He does not just paint the flattering picture required by the usual sitter. He portrays the character as well as the likeness. I have watched the

[1] See the illustration facing page 164.

progress of some of his portraits during our long talks together. I remember on one occasion he told me what a 'sweet, charming, warm-hearted' person his model was, for his first impulse on meeting someone is to look for their likeable qualities and ignore the others. But gradually as the picture progressed, we both saw how the real man emerged, and became aware of a streak of ruthless egotism which was in fact the strongest trait of his character. In 1951, as Christ Church wanted a portrait of Anthony Eden, I offered to have him painted by Kokoschka. But Eden could not spare the time for the sittings required, so unfortunately nothing came of the suggestion. I am sorry about this as Oskar would have done a wonderful portrait, and at that time he was badly in need of money.

All my life I have bought contemporary paintings, often by artists unknown at the time, many of whom like Oskar have since become famous. Friends have sometimes asked me what were the qualities I looked for in selecting these pictures and I think I could summarise them under three general headings. In the first place, to my mind, the artist must be sufficiently original, so that a glance at his pictures convinces you they are by him and no one else. A Kokoschka, a Picasso, a Stanley Spencer, a Dali have peculiarities of their own that prevent them from being confused with the work of other painters.

Next I look for a first-class technique. For this reason I would exclude such a well-known painter as Bernard Buffet, who certainly passes test No. 1 for originality. But I find his colour dismal, with no variety or subtlety. Whether in drawing, sketch or finished painting, 'the touch of the master' implies the highest degree of craftsmanship.

The third quality I look for, namely taste, is the most difficult to assess, as it depends so much on your own perceptiveness. The originality and craftsmanship must be blended with a certain refinement and harmony; to me it then becomes a work of art.

I think an artist should only be judged by his best works, and a collector should then try to acquire only these.

British art galleries suffer a great disadvantage compared with most American ones: they are never allowed to sell any of their pictures. This prevents their disposing of works of secondary importance and, with the revenue thus obtained, gradually improving the standard of their exhibits.

The late Pierpont Morgan, during his lifetime, was often denigrated by his business associates for the high prices he paid to build up his collection of pictures. But in fact he got excellent advice and only bought the best. When on leave during the last war I was able to attend the sale of his collection. Whereas his enormous banking and industrial shareholding had greatly fallen in value, his picture collection, despite the war, was sold at enormously higher prices than their cost, because they included the finest paintings each artist had produced.

I have always bought pictures at the time they were painted for the sheer pleasure they gave me, and I think I must have given away to my friends more pictures than I now possess. Years ago I often used to give Picasso drawings, then costing about twenty pounds, as wedding presents. It is only since the last war that contemporary paintings have risen to such enormously high prices. This is because Americans are now allowed to pay for a picture as a deduction from high taxes, if donated to a museum after death. They are therefore able to adorn their walls at the American government's expense. Hence, for millionaires in the higher tax bracket in the U.S.A., the price does not matter.

All this has led to great speculation in works of art. As one French dealer pointed out, 'Everyone wants to discover a new winner, whose prices, like Renoir and Van Gogh, will rocket in the future.' These speculations may go badly astray. My grandfather used to pay a high price for a Millais picture, which today has a negligible value. I wonder how many of the fashionable abstract painters of today will survive even twenty years from now?

Quite apart from my pleasure in Oskar's company, I am enthusiastic about his paintings because they fulfil just those qualities I especially admire. In fact he once paid me the compliment of saying that of all his friends no one understood the 'best' of his work more truly than I did.

During Oskar's stay in Zermatt, he had of course met my old friend and guide William Perren, who often helped him to carry his easel to places, secret to them both, where William would watch Oskar painting the mountains they both love so dearly. When Oskar came back to England we talked a great deal about William and the way he represented, like Oskar himself, the type of man who remains untouched by the lure of materialism.

Since the age of thirty I had spent most of my holidays in William's company, ski-ing in the winter and walking and mountain-climbing in summer. At the beginning of the war, before returning to his Alpine regiment, and feeling perhaps that we might never meet again, he had written me a beautiful letter: 'Thank you very much for all you have done for me and my people. Whatever happens I shall always think of you, thank you and pray for you. Yours truly, even to the bitter end, William.'

It was wonderful after the war being together again. William, like me, is tremendously strong, so we have been well matched for the climbs and arduous expeditions we have enjoyed together. He is tall, with a finely-hewn face, deeply-lined by the sun and cold of the mountains. He has a thick mass of jet-black hair, now streaked with grey, and a gentle look in his dark, heavily-lidded eyes. He loves and venerates the mountains. His keen awareness and delight in every different facet of nature quickens one's own perception, for he is always calling one's attention to some flower or some effect of light on the mountain landscape, or in winter marking the track of hare, chamois or fox in the snow. Out ski-ing I have never met his equal in selecting the best line of country, or the slope where snow conditions are most favourable. He it was who taught me the pleasure of summer ski-ing, only possible at altitudes above 10,000 feet, over glaciers covered with snow.

William's family has owned land in and around Zermatt from time immemorial. He once showed me the date 1554 over the door of one of his primitive wooden chalets right up near the glaciers. Besides being, like his father, a mountain guide, he has continued, with the help of his family, to look after his cattle and his various small pieces of land, none of which he would ever dream of selling, however hard up he might be. There is a great contrast between his way of farming and what we are used to in England. He, his wife or children, would think nothing of climbing some 1,200 feet at dawn to milk the cows, and then bringing down the milk in cans strapped to their backs. Crops of hay or oats are cut with a scythe and carried long distances in immense baskets. No mules or tractors were used in Zermatt when I first knew him, and great was his delight when one summer I gave him a small hand-tractor.

William is also a highly skilled carpenter. Before he began to build his new house, I remember how he showed me some particularly tall pine trees. 'This one will become the staircase, these two will be for the floorboards, and that one over there I shall use for the balconies.' The trees, which are communally owned in Zermatt, were cut and brought down in winter across the snow. He then set to work breaking up the stones for the foundations, carrying the sand from a small piece of river-bed which he owned, and mixing the cement. The whole house was built entirely by himself, the only outside help being for the plumbing, bath and sanitary arrangements.

William is deeply religious. Every morning and evening, without fail, he attends church. Once, in a cabin high up in the mountains which we had reached at dusk, he asked me if

I minded not beginning our climb before eight o'clock the next morning. I agreed, thinking he was tired and wanted a lie-in because it was Sunday. It was only later that I found out that he had left at 3 a.m. and gone down to early Mass in the village, climbing back again for three hours to be in time for me. Guides of his generation in Zermatt, with their lives constantly in danger, would not wish to have on their conscience their absence from Mass on Sundays.

William has not prospered like so many other guides in Zermatt, who have started shops or small hotels, and so taken advantage of the enormous increase in the number of tourists in the village. He could never envisage life except as a free man, earning his living by helping his 'clients' to enjoy 'his' beloved mountains. His values are not money values. I once discovered that he had allowed a family, to whom he had let a flat in his chalet, to continue to occupy it although they had not paid their rent for a year. He said he felt sorry for them and could not bear to turn them out or bring pressure on them in order to be paid, because he knew they were in financial difficulties.

Before the war William and I were in the Engadine and Quintin Hogg and his brother Neil joined us in some climbing. Quintin, when he was a young man, was not very good at taking advice, and would not listen to me when I suggested that he should put on a shirt when he had to cross a mere hundred yards of snow. With the result that he got so badly sunburned he had to lie in a cold bath, filled with as much bicarbonate-of-soda as we could raise locally, and have ice packs on the very sore parts.

When he recovered we all went up the Pitz Palu, one of the most beautiful mountains in Switzerland above the 4,000-metre line. We had an arduous walk up to the Diavolessa Hut the first night, and started our climb up next morning an hour before dawn. The last part along the *arête* is impossible in very windy weather. In places it is only about two feet wide, with a drop of thousands of feet down on both the Swiss and Italian sides. But there was no wind, and conditions were perfect. On the summit we got out the 'visitors' book from under the heavy stone where it lay and all signed our names. The summit is only about six feet wide and William suggested this was a nice place to have a quiet lunch. But looking down the precipitous slopes on either side had a bad effect on my appetite, and we had lunch a little later on!

For me, the thought of William will always recall happy memories. I used to ring up Zermatt and ask, 'How's the snow?' and if the answer was satisfactory, off I would go, sometimes just for a weekend, to speed down the steep, white slopes in the beautiful sunshine. For a long time before I had my chalet at Zermatt, Sestrières was my favourite weekend ski-ing haunt. I could fly to Paris at five o'clock on a Friday afternoon, take a sleeper and arrive at eight o'clock in the morning at Sestrières, dressed in ski-ing clothes. William would meet me at the station with my skis. We would ski all Saturday and Sunday, and I would be back in the City on Monday morning. With youthful enthusiasm William and I once tried to see how many feet descent in height we could do in two days. We managed over 50,000 feet one weekend, or more than twice the height of Mont Blanc.

In the winter before the war William trained me most carefully for what proved to be my last ski-ing race on the Corviglia Standard run at St Moritz. I raced, among others, against the British Olympic team which included such fine skiers as Billy Clyde, Roger Bushell, Paddy Green and Mouse Cleaver. My time of two minutes forty seconds was under twenty seconds after the winner, which at forty years of age was a tribute to William's skill as a trainer.

Besides visiting me himself, two of William's sons have stayed for months at my farm in England to learn English, and the third and eldest one whom I had trained as an English chartered accountant now has a high, executive position in Zürich. My son Serge was taught by William to ski from the age of three, and great was William's pride when his pupil achieved Gold Medal standard at twelve years of age. So William and I are bound together by many close ties, which have woven a pattern of intimate friendship through our lives.

And it was only natural that walking one day up the mountain paths, I should have confided to him how for many years my marriage to Irina had conformed to the old saying of 'Marry in haste and repent at leisure'. I could not interest her in my aims and activities, nor could she understand and share my values; and we had slowly drifted apart. I have had enough experience of the world to realise that if the personalities of a married couple are incompatible it is wrong to put the blame on one side or the other; I had also come to the conclusion that it was better to live alone by oneself, than to live alone in the married state, so the time came when we decided to separate. A year later Irina asked me to divorce her so that she could remarry. I am glad to say she is now very happy and has two more children.

These had been sad and trying years; for my fervent desire for a happy home life had not been realised. The result had been to make me throw all my efforts into work. At one time I spent some months translating a very fine French novel, living quietly alone in my chalet in Zermatt, and found this exercise a splendid discipline for the mind, since at a 'dead period' in life it forced me into a state of complete detachment. No doubt it is for this reason that many writers, between moments of creative activity, have undertaken laborious translations.

The combination of walks with William, the ever-changing beauty of the mountain scenery, the pleasure I derived through being in contact with the mind of a fine writer by translating his work, greatly helped me to resolve my own problems.

Chapter Thirteen

★

THE EUROPEAN MOVEMENT

W INSTON Churchill, looking at the future from the vantage point of a historian, and one who had himself so greatly influenced the history of his time, said in his famous speech at Zürich University in 1946, 'When the Nazi power was broken I asked myself what was the best advice I could give my fellow citizens in our ravaged and exhausted continent. My counsel to Europe can be given in a single word: Unite!' He then put forward a comprehensive programme for the creation of a united Europe.

This conception made a great appeal to me. I felt it was not a nebulous ideal. It was a concrete and practical policy which I believed might be realised in a not too distant future. Henceforth more and more of my time and energies were to be devoted to this cause.

Shortly after Zürich Sir Winston Churchill created the United Europe Movement, and I was invited to join the committee, which included Mr Harold Macmillan, Bob Boothby (now Lord Boothby), David Maxwell Fyfe (now Viscount Kilmuir), Lady Violet Bonham Carter, Lord Layton, with Mr Duncan Sandys and Lady Rhys Williams as its very active secretaries. The committee met regularly in Sir Winston's private room in the House of Commons, and planned to spread the idea both in England and in Europe.

About that time I met Senator Van Zeeland, former Prime Minister of Belgium, and gave a dinner in London for him to explain his views on the economic position in

Europe. He made a most moving speech in English, without notes, with an eloquence rare even amongst the finest British orators I have heard. It sometimes happens, as with Conrad, whose mother tongue was Polish, that when a foreigner has really mastered English, he brings to our language all the imagery and colour of his own.

Picturing the terrible economic plight of continental Europe, devastated by the war, he urged us all to co-operate to meet the grave situation. This led to the formation of the European League for Economic Co-Operation (E.L.E.C.) with himself as president, and its headquarters in Brussels. E.L.E.C. was a group of politicians, economists, trade-unionists and business-men, and unlike the United Europe Movement, its aim was not propaganda, but to prepare carefully-considered plans to meet economic problems. I helped to set up the British committee, asking my old friend of I.L.O. days, Sir Harold Butler, to be chairman. We were careful to make it all-party.

Its first important opportunity occurred the day after General Marshall had announced, in vague terms, the generous offer of American aid for Europe. An E.L.E.C. committee, under Lord Layton, immediately met in Paris and drafted concrete proposals to the British, French and American governments outlining how this lavish generosity could be channelled along constructive lines. It thus made a very practical contribution to the elaboration of the Marshall Plan.

Among many other achievements of E.L.E.C. were proposals for the convertibility of European currencies, suggested by its monetary committee in November 1949. This became the blueprint of the European Payments Union. The committee included Sir David Eccles, Sir Roy Harrod, M. Janssen (former Finance Minister of Belgium), Lord Layton, M. Monick (Hon. Governor of the Bank of France), Mr Paul Chambers, with myself as chairman.

Sir Roy Harrod prepared the original draft of this plan

and the conception was entirely his. I feel he has never received the credit due to him for the creation of the European Payments Union, which was such an important factor in the economic revival of the fifties.

I cannot even briefly mention the activities of the British section of E.L.E.C. without paying a tribute to Lady Rhys Williams, D.B.E., its honorary secretary from its inception to the present day. Few people realise how much work is involved in running such a voluntary organisation. You have to urge members to come to committee-meetings and go to conferences abroad. You have to arrange to have technical papers prepared. You have to consult the various government departments or even cabinet ministers on some of the problems involved. You also have to be careful never to bring important people to a gathering without the agenda being well thought out and interesting enough for all to be able to make a useful contribution. Juliet is one of those dedicated women who devote themselves to a cause with selfless enthusiasm and indefatigable energy.

On the Continent other organisations came into being with the general object of furthering European unity, but many of these activities overlapped and proved a weakness to the general cause. It was due to the initiative of Duncan Sandys, that whilst retaining their separate status, these organisations grouped themselves into the European Movement which became the parent body, with Sir Winston Churchill and Robert Schuman as its presidents. In this way the European Movement became a super-political pressure-group which has already greatly influenced the course of European history.

Only those who worked in the early days of the Movement realise that the driving force that created it was largely British, as well as the money which financed it. Lord McGowan, chairman of Imperial Chemical Industries, assisted by his new recruit from the Treasury, Paul Chambers, would gather together leaders of British industry at a luncheon in Sir Winston's honour, and would then ask for generous donations for the European cause. This was readily given in homage to the greatest Englishman of our time.

As Sir Winston's lieutenant, Duncan Sandys, chairman of the movement's executive committee, was indefatigable, going from one country to another, drafting and redrafting documents, refusing to accept defeat, overcoming opposition by his persistence, and compelling admiration by his devotion to the cause.

These activities led up to the Congress of The Hague in 1948, which created the Consultative Assembly of Strasbourg, and laid the foundations of the Common Market, Euratom and the Coal and Steel Community.

I will not deal with the events of this conference which have so often been recorded. At that time, air travel in Europe was rather elementary, so I gave a lift home from The Hague to some of my fellow delegates in a Dove, a private plane which I often used. The passengers were Lady Violet Bonham Carter, Lord Layton, Sir Harold Butler, Harold Macmillan and Peter Thorneycroft. All went well until we arrived over Croydon, when the aeroplane kept circling round in the air without landing. Looking down we saw great activity on the airfield in the shape of numerous Red Cross ambulances, and fire-fighting apparatus. The pilot explained that the undercarriage would not open, and that he was staying up in the air until he had used up the petrol, so he could make a belly-flop landing. He told us to crowd to the back of the plane when he landed to help to balance its nose. I was especially worried knowing that Irina was waiting below and would be made very anxious by all the preparations, and wished I had not asked my friends to share what might prove a most unpleasant experience. But everything worked out happily. After an hour's cruising about, the aircraft made a safe landing, turned on its nose, and we jumped out safely.

We celebrated our escape with a sumptuous champagne lunch at my home. Harold was in high spirits, and jovially remarked, 'Everybody behaved as English gentlemen should behave on such occasions. Lord Layton was discussing with Lady Violet the future of the Liberal Party, as if they were sitting at ease on the terrace of the House of Commons. Butler was discussing some intricate passage of The Hague resolutions with Peter Thorneycroft, Edward, our host, was apologising to the rest of us for having perhaps to put us to some inconvenience on landing, and was most disturbed for us in case it might upset our plans.' He went on to tell of an accident he had had under similar circumstances, when his aeroplane caught fire on landing in Algiers during the war, and he was badly hurt. He mentioned that a Free-French admiral, who had jumped out with him, and lost his hat with his admiral's badges, kept calling for 'Mon chapeau, mon chapeau', and was with difficulty restrained from returning to the burning plane to fetch this sole emblem of his authority.

We donated a gold cigarette-case to our pilot, Wing-Commander Mallorie, for his splendid handling of the plane. But after that experience I ceased using private planes and confined myself to flying on the regular routes.

The next occasion on which the United Europe Committee met was one day in Sir Winston's room in the House of Commons. He was to lead a delegation of us to see Mr Attlee in order to place before him the resolutions passed at The Hague Conference. Sir Winston was in his jauntiest mood, smoking his large cigar, and making amusing personal remarks to his friends. We marched from the House of Commons with him in the lead. Crossing the road into Whitehall, the policeman on duty, with a twinkle in his eye, held up the traffic perhaps even for a few moments longer than necessary. People stopped in the street and began to gaze at the strange sight of the great Churchill marching at the head of his little platoon. There were

N

occasional cheers and smiling faces in response to his greeting with his right hand uplifted in the 'V' sign.

It was a very solemn occasion when we sat down in the cabinet room at 10 Downing Street. Mr Attlee and members of his cabinet were on one side of the table and Sir Winston and his delegation on the other. As Attlee and Sir Winston had been in the cabinet together during all the war years, I naturally expected them to call each other by their Christian names and discuss their business in a friendly informal manner. But this was not at all what happened. Churchill started off in a stately and formal tone of voice, addressing himself to 'Mr Prime Minister' and 'humbly' laying before him 'the resolutions of The Hague Conference'. Very slowly, choosing his words, generally using three adjectives at a time, he spoke of the 'cruel, devastating, heart-rending' misery caused by the war and the need of a united Europe as the only constructive policy for the future.

In opening the discussion Mr Attlee mentioned the great honour he had enjoyed in serving under the greatest Prime Minister in British history; and the members of the Labour government, with Mr Bevin, the Foreign Secretary, took great pains to show that they could rise to the standard set by Churchill in the exchange of personal courtesies with their political opponents.

Refugee delegates from the countries behind the Iron Curtain had attended The Hague Conference, and some of them came to the European Movement's Economic Conference held at Church House in 1949. On this occasion Randolph Churchill asked me to a little luncheon he was giving for them. Some had been prime ministers, and all had held leading positions in their own countries, until recently. Randolph felt sorry for them as we all did. Most were in straitened circumstances, and were weighed down by the tragedies that had swept over their homelands. But pity is not a good basis for friendship or active co-operation. What was wanted was to find a practical means of getting them to work together in support of their enslaved countrymen, with the active help of those in the West who believed in their cause.

As a result of talks with Harold Macmillan and with the help of Joseph Retinger, a Polish patriot, who knew all the leading personalities in the countries behind the Iron Curtain, we set up the Central and Eastern European Commission of the European Movement. Its object was to uphold the right of individual and political freedom for the countries under Soviet domination in Eastern Europe and urge their inclusion in a future United Europe. Mr Harold Macmillan was chairman and I was *rapporteur* of this committee, which included exiled personalities from Bulgaria, Czechoslovakia, Hungary, Poland, Rumania and Yugoslavia; also two former French prime ministers, Paul Ramadier and Paul Reynaud. The British representatives were Julian Amery, Clement Davies, and my old friend Arthur Greenwood, representing the three political parties. On the lines of the other pressure-groups with which I had been concerned, we prepared a pamphlet called *A Basis for an Eastern European Policy*, setting out the kind of economic policies and political programme that would prove practical if these countries were free to choose their own destiny. This report, which was the subject of endless discussions in London, Paris and Strasbourg, was also endorsed by all the most prominent exiled leaders not members of the Commission. It thus proved a rallying-point for focussing the political ideas of the exiles along lines on which general agreement was possible. All this demanded a great deal of work and the Commission was housed in my offices in Park Lane, with George Morton and John Pomian as joint secretaries. Pomian was a Pole who had served in the R.A.F., and was part-time secretary to Retinger. Morton spoke German, French and Italian fluently and had won a D.S.O. for parachuting into Italy under Colin Gubbins's command. Working side by side in the same office we became close friends. It took a great deal of tact and patience on the part of our little team to deal with some of the problems posed by those whom Harold Macmillan, in friendly and jocular terms, called 'the bandits'!

Harold Macmillan was a splendid person to work with. He never pushed himself forward or tried to get the lime-light, as so many politicians I had known. He told me he would like to join E.L.E.C. 'I don't want any prominent position on the committee. I believe you are doing valuable work and would like to help in any modest way I can.' When things went well he would give the credit to others, though we all knew it was largely due to his initiative. He is a marvellous listener, and when at some meeting I would get impatient with many of the views expressed, he would say, 'Let them talk themselves out'. In the end he would rise from his chair, pay a tribute to the different views expressed, and put forward his own contrary ones in such a friendly and moderate way that they would be accepted.

He once told me that he had the best training in diplomacy in his own publishing business, for authors are sometimes more difficult to manage than politicians.

At one rather stormy meeting of the European Movement, Paul-Henri Spaak got up in a fury and said he would leave the meeting. Many rushed out to beg him to return, but Macmillan said quietly to me, 'Don't worry, he will soon be back. If he really wanted to leave he would have gone out by the door on the right. He went out by the door on the left leading to the cloakroom!' And in fact he soon returned.

Macmillan was an indefatigable worker, always willing to correct drafts, and dealing quickly and efficiently with his correspondence. Even now, when as Prime Minister he is overwhelmed with work, I receive answers to my letters more promptly than from any of my business friends.

The way he espoused the cause of the 'bandits' was an example of his capacity for devotion to a principle he believed in. He could gain no credit in home politics for his championship of this cause. It was very unpopular with the Foreign Office; and public opinion in most Western countries was too hardened by what had happened in the last war to care deeply for injustice not actually paraded before its eyes. But Macmillan felt it was an article of faith for the Western world to continue to declare that these people should have the right to enjoy personal liberty and national freedom. He finally persuaded the Consultative Assembly of the Council of Europe at Strasbourg to set up a 'special committee to watch over the interests of the countries not represented on the Council of Europe'. This Committee, of which he eventually became chairman, was composed of Western European parliamentary delegates to the Assembly. It still functions today, and constitutes a tangible proof, for the people behind the Iron Curtain, that their cause is still upheld by their fellow Europeans in the West.

Over ten years ago, there occurred an event which I believe will be considered of great significance when historians of the future study the evolution towards European unity. In May 1951 E.L.E.C. organised a Commonwealth Europe Conference under the chairmanship of Mr Macmillan. This conference was attended by leading economic and academic personalities from each of the dominions and from each European country. They discussed the problems of closer economic integration between the Commonwealth and Europe. We first had three days of discussions in London amongst British and Commonwealth delegates, followed by a larger conference in Brussels with our European colleagues. In London we were at sixes and sevens, as so often happens in family discussions. But once in Brussels, the British and Commonwealth delegates made a common front in full agreement when faced with the views of the Continental representatives.

The important conclusion of the conference was that there need be no incompatibility between greater integration of Britain with Europe, and Britain's close relationship with the Commonwealth. Everyone would benefit immeasurably. This was the view taken by Mr Macmillan when ten years later, as Prime Minister, he made a formal application for Britain to join the Common Market.

When the Conservatives won the election in the autumn of 1951, their British colleagues on the European Movement were left in rather a quandary. It seemed as if a section of the Conservative Party, headed by Anthony Eden, were opposed to closer ties between Britain and Europe, and had been powerful enough to influence Winston Churchill in the selection of the posts in his new government. None of those who had been associated with him in his United Europe adventure, like Harold Macmillan, Maxwell Fyfe, Duncan Sandys, David Eccles and Peter Thorneycroft, had any position in the government connected with Foreign Affairs. The Grand Fighter, in his old age, seemed to have been thwarted by the less forward-looking wing of his party.

I soon found evidence of this in even greater hostility from the Foreign Office to our European activities, especially to our idea of holding an Eastern European Conference in January 1952. This was our most ambitious plan so far. One of my personal difficulties was to persuade all sections of Poles to attend, for there was a deep feud between the Polish refugee government and Mr Mikołajczyk, head of the Polish Peasant Party. He had been Vice-Premier of Poland in a coalition Communist-controlled government until he was obliged to flee the country. Like King Michael of Rumania, he had tried to work under a Communist régime in the hope of saving some measure of liberty for his countrymen. But so great was the desire of all the exiles to attend this conference, that finally a reconciliation took place. In the end, despite Foreign Office opposition, Winston Churchill gave us his personal encouragement and Harold Macmillan stood staunchly by his friends, so despite everything, we held the conference after all.

It proved a great success and Harold Macmillan spoke at the opening session welcoming the delegates on behalf of the government, and at a dinner I gave on the first evening. He and Duncan Sandys also sat on the platform at a mass-meeting in the Albert Hall on the closing night of the conference. The organisation of such a large meeting had been quite a problem, and I was greatly relieved, when I got up to propose the resolution, that it was before a packed house. After referring to the gallantry of the Poles and Czechs who had fought by our side in the last war, I came to our resolution, which was passed with acclamation. It stated that 'No arrangement between the Western Powers and the Soviet Union can lead to a true and lasting peace which accepts the continued enslavement of the peoples of Central and Eastern Europe'. I am convinced that this declaration is still applicable today, for if circumstances change to enable Soviet Russia and the West to live side by side in peaceful amity, the Soviet will no longer need to maintain these populations under their enslaved rule.

The success of the conference, whose views were put over the air by all the European radio-stations and the powerful American Freedom Radio of Munich, may be gauged by the fierceness of the Soviet response. For weeks and weeks the conference was denounced by the Russian radio and press, and by the puppet leaders of the countries behind the Iron Curtain.

The supporters in England of the idea of a United Europe were disheartened by the failure of Mr Churchill's government to pursue the European policy he had inspired. Many of us, however, were convinced that it was the only long-term policy for Britain, and continued all the more arduously to promote its general aims. I myself decided gradually to resign from most of my industrial chairmanships so that I could give ever more time to this work. I had found a cause I completely believed in, to which my personal experience and energies could make a contribution. I had also learnt from life that if you believe strongly in an ideal, it is not the actual attainment of that ideal within a given time that matters, but striving and fighting for it. You are thus not discouraged by disappointment, which on the contrary often acts as a spur to greater effort.

Since the war the British government's European policy appears always to have been the right one, but invariably a few years too late. It seems only yesterday that Mr Paul-Henri Spaak was saying to me, before the signing of the Treaty of Rome, that if Britain would only join the Common Market, she could write her own terms. But the British government even withdrew our observer, the very able Mr Bretherton, from these negotiations, thinking nothing would come of them. When Mr Harold Macmillan became Prime Minister, the position could not be reversed, for the Treaty of Rome had already been signed.

As soon as the Common Market was formed, the international organisation of the European Movement (forgetting its origins at The Hague Conference, calling for the unity of *all* Europe) ceased to be concerned with any activities outside the problem of the six Common Market countries. Its new chairman, M. Robert Schuman, growing old, and overwhelmed with other responsibilities, could not give the movement the leadership it required. The United Kingdom Council of the movement, which had elected me to be its chairman, therefore decided to continue its own campaign in favour of the unity of all the free countries this side of the Iron Curtain, as well as a long-term educative programme at home to make the problems of Britain's closer links with Europe better understood by the public at large.

In every similar political 'pressure-group' with which I have been connected, I have always advocated an all-party approach. On this Council, leading members of the Labour Party — like Alfred Robens, Denis Healey, Reggie Paget, Arthur Bottomley and Bob Edwards, and Lord Layton for the Liberal Party — contributed equally with Conser-

Churchill's last public speech at Central Hall, Westminster, 1957

vatives like Bob Boothby, Sir James Hutchison, Maurice Macmillan, Lady Horsbrugh and Geoffrey Rippon. We felt that our main task was not merely to rally the converted, but to convince the enormous body of the so-called 'uncommitted'. We also tried to popularise the idea in employers' and trade-union circles.

Just as the European Movement on the Continent had originally brought together independent groups, a further aim of the United Kingdom Council was to unite all societies advocating a new European policy, such as the United Europe Movement and the British Section of E.L.E.C. The Council also included bodies like Federal Union, whose views on political integration were far in advance of what was politically acceptable at the time, and for this reason often made a greater appeal to youth. History has proved that the preaching of what at one moment is thought of as an extreme policy often contributes to make a more moderate one, moving in the same direction, meet with eventual acceptance.

One morning in July 1957 I went to see Sir Winston Churchill at his house, to discuss the speech he was going to make at a great meeting of the European Movement that evening at the Central Hall, Westminster. The meeting was to inaugurate a campaign to make better known the problems of the Free Trade Area and the Common Market.

I was wondering how I would find him as I had not seen him for several years; and since then he had been very ill and had retired from being Prime Minister. Miss Revel-Guest, who was one of the organisers of the meeting and a Parliamentary candidate, begged me to let her accompany me, as she was particularly anxious to meet the great Churchill in person. But he sent a message that he could not receive her as he was in bed.

Apart from an old servant, he seemed alone in the house, He had on very beautiful, bright yellow, Chinese silk pyjamas, decorated with black dragons. He was smoking a cigar and there was some brandy by his side. He was sitting up in bed and there was a fitted tray over his knees, on which were some notes for the evening meeting. He seemed in a dour and worried mood; but with his usual old-time courtesy he asked me if I would have some whisky, brandy, or some orange juice, or a cigar, which I politely refused.

We then came to discuss his speech for the evening. He showed me the notes which had been prepared, but which seemed to me not quite suitable to the occasion. I explained to him that as the meeting was also going to be addressed by leading Frenchmen and Germans, it might be desirable that his theme, which would be widely publicised on the Continent, should be a message to Europe on the lines of his original Zürich speech, stressing the need for unity. I mentioned that I thought this line would also be helpful to the Prime Minister, as Britain had been accused of reverting to an insular policy because of her refusal to join the Common Market. He looked up at me and suddenly growled: 'I don't know if I want to help Harold. Perhaps he is going too far.'

My first feeling was one of astonishment, but I soon realised that he had no wish to oppose Macmillan or throw a spanner in the mechanism of our conference. His pugnacious reaction was not directed against me but against his own infirmities. In the olden days, one had to be on one's toes when putting forward any views in his presence. He was so quick at repartee; like a flash one might be tripped up, or he would take a side theme and astound one by the brilliance of his eloquence and thought. But here was a Samson shorn of his locks, and speaking to him one had to utter one's words very slowly and wait a minute or so for a reply. Slowly he asked: 'Did I say this at Zürich?' 'I was founder of the European Movement, wasn't I?' I felt terribly sorry for him.

He asked me to write out a draft for his speech, which I did, emphasising a point I felt was desirable to put over;

namely, that the formation of the Six was one stage in the movement towards the integration of Europe, but that alone it might divide Europe into two blocks unless it was followed by a close association with other free countries in Europe. When he had heard it he said: 'All this is too complicated. I am out of touch with events today. I cannot remember things clearly any more.' However, he asked me to send the draft to Duncan Sandys at once and ask him to work on it. He was extremely courteous when I left and said, 'Would you please extend my warm regards to the lady who came with you and express my sincere regrets that I was unable to see her.'

I immediately rang up Duncan Sandys at a cabinet meeting, and explained the position to him. He cancelled all other appointments, and redrafted my modest notes into Churchillian style.

That evening I met Churchill at the entrance to the Central Hall. He looked very tired and weary and I felt anxious about the outcome. It was a great day for me to preside at a meeting and to have Mr Harold Macmillan, the Prime Minister, on my right, and Sir Winston Churchill on my left. On the platform were the Archbishop of Canterbury, nearly all the members of the government, and some of the most distinguished personalities in the country. But my thoughts were for Churchill. He seemed so tired and exhausted, and in a very nervous state. Just before I got up he asked me, 'How long will you be?' I had prepared a very carefully worded speech for this important occasion. But at such a moment Churchill came before everything, and to put his mind at rest I immediately decided to discard my speech and instead replied, 'One minute', which was the time I gave myself to welcome the greatest Englishman in my lifetime. He got up to deliver the last oration he was to make in public for a cause whose origin owed so much to his inspiring call to action in previous years. It lasted five minutes, and standing up he put into it all his strength, all his courage and determination. His voice was powerful, as of old. He made a pause here and there at the appropriate moment, for the anticipated applause. It recalled the Churchill who had stirred the free world in the tragic moments of our history. It was a great personal triumph, but few of those present that evening realised, as I did, the superhuman effort it required.

In 1957 Britain had put forward the idea of a European Free Trade Area, which differs from a Customs Union in that its members, whilst abolishing tariffs as between themselves, retain their own tariffs against the outside world. The British government hoped that this Free Trade Area would form an outer circle linking itself with the six Common Market countries.

The United Kingdom Council of the European Movement had for some time been organising regional meetings, where members of the government and of the Labour Party had discussed in detail the problems of the proposed Free Trade Area with the local trade-unions and industrial leaders. The meetings had been a great success, and Alfred Robens and others on our council conceived the idea of our organising a European Industrial Conference solely of trade-unionists and employers, to discuss these problems.

The technique of organising an international conference of this kind is not very different from that of negotiating an important amalgamation between large industrial companies, a procedure with which I am familiar. You have to get one element after another to agree to the original plan, and then further acceptances snowball. But the preliminary moves always present the main difficulty.

I first got government approval and the promise that if the conference took place the Chancellor of the Exchequer would open it. The government was naturally in favour of any initiative that would help to overcome the general apathy that prevailed about these European problems.

Alfred Robens obtained similar assurances from the Labour Party. The British employers' organisations were, however, extremely lukewarm on the idea of a conference, preferring to organise their own conference confined to their close associates. I got over this initial difficulty by forming a panel of prominent British industrialists, not closely-linked with the employers' organisations, who were prepared to act as sponsors for the employers' side of the conference. Lord Knollys was the chairman of this panel, which included Lord Godber, chairman of Shell, Lord Chandos and Sir Eric Bowater.

Our director, Sir Archibald Gordon, who had previously held a high position at the Ministry of Labour, arranged a dinner at my club with some leading members of the Trades Union Congress (who included Mr Alan Birch, chairman of their Economic Committee), and many helpful suggestions were made. However, the T.U.C., influenced to some extent by the employers' organisations, would not give formal approval until the attitude of the continental trade-unionists was determined.

In the meantime, it was decided to make the purpose of the conference a free discussion of the problems of the Common Market and the proposal for it to be associated with a Free Trade Area, without the passing of resolutions. Too much time is generally wasted at international conferences in discussing resolutions which are eventually so watered-down to meet opposing views that they have little impact on public opinion. A free discussion by delegates approaching problems with an open mind was a better way of securing a wider circle of delegates and influencing the 'uncommitted'.

The next move was to visit various countries on the Continent to sound out opinions and attitudes. In view of the negative attitude of some of the British employers' organisations, strong support from abroad was needed to ensure success.

My old friend, the Polish patriot, Dr Joseph Retinger, who had been working tirelessly to further the European cause, ever since The Hague Conference, offered to help me. He had become famous during the war for his parachute drop, at fifty-six years of age, into occupied Poland, and the dramatic circumstances of his return to England. After his beloved Poland was annexed by Russia and he saw he could no longer be useful there, he devoted himself to the great idea of the creation of a united Europe. He was a selfless, dedicated man who never put himself forward but was content to bring together men whom he believed would share his ideals and would work to further his creative political conceptions. He was that very rare kind of person, a 'political promoter'. Once a new idea was launched and had taken root, he was content to help it along actively from the sidelines, leaving to others the limelight of actual leadership. Unlike 'business promoters', he wanted neither material gain nor personal glory; his recompense was the success of the cause he had at heart. He had helped Churchill to found the European Movement and inspired the creation of the European League for Economic Co-operation, as well as the Central and Eastern European Commission of the European Movement.

His friendships in high places were extraordinary. Ten years previously I had gone to America with him and Duncan Sandys to try to form an American committee of supporters for the European Movement. To my great surprise, on his arrival in New York, Retinger picked up the telephone in our sitting-room at the Plaza Hotel, and spoke directly to President Truman and then to General Marshall, and made immediate appointments to see them. In Europe he had the *entrée* into every political circle, as a kind of right acquired through the devotion and loyalty he inspired.

Despite his being slightly crippled, and in very delicate health, he insisted on accompanying me on my initial visit to Scandinavia. Our first place of call was Stockholm where, thanks to Retinger's arrangements, we were immediately received by Mr Tage Erlander, the Socialist Prime Minister, who promised to attend the conference in his private capacity, so as to become better acquainted with the problems involved.

Having secured such welcome support from the Prime Minister, our task in Sweden was made easy, especially as Sir Robert Hankey, our ambassador, introduced us to many people who were able to help us. We were welcomed by Mr Aman, M.P., head of the 'white collar' union, and Mr Geiger, M.P., chairman of the Swedish T.U.C. and of the International Confederation of Free Trades Unions, who arranged that the Confederation should instruct its members in other countries to give every support to our conference. Mr Aman's union was unique by British standards, for it encompassed all those in government service, including the army and navy and all its officers. In fact, salary and wage agreements in Sweden seem to be based on a most satisfactory and stable basis, compared with the free-for-all procedure in other countries. They are negotiated by a joint committee of representatives of the government, the trade-unions and the employers and cover everybody; so industrial strife is very rare and the friendliest relations exist between the employers and trade-union organisations.

Mr Mark Wallenberg, the leading banker and industrialist in Sweden, assured the support of Swedish employers. We felt it was also wise to call on leaders of the opposition parties, and saw Dr Bertil Ohlin, head of the Liberal Party, whom we had met previously at the Council of Europe at Strasbourg. He promised not to force a new government crisis during the time of the proposed visit of the Prime Minister to London!

Our visit to Norway was equally successful. We called on Mr Gerhardson, the Prime Minister, who, speaking through an interpreter, strongly endorsed the idea of the conference and told me how much Norway sympathised with British

policy on economic affairs. In fact, I found the atmosphere
in Norway rather like that of New Zealand, where the feeling
is more pro-English even than in Great Britain. In Oslo, if
you go into most booksellers, you may find the front of the
shop full of English books and only at the back will you see
books in Norwegian.

Having got the Norwegian Prime Minister's endorsement,
trade-unionists and employers promised full co-operation.
In fact, the view generally expressed in Sweden and Norway
was that the solidarity of these two countries with Britain at
this unofficial conference in London, might have a helpful
psychological repercussion on the Free Trade Area discussions with the Common Market.

Denmark's position was different to that of her other two
Scandinavian partners, for though she sold some 46 per cent
of her exports to Britain, she badly needed the Continental
market. But Danish support was equally forthcoming. We
discussed the position with Mr Krag, the Minister of
Economic Affairs, with the opposition leader Mr Kraft,
head of the Conservative Party, and my old friend Mr Per
Federspiel, chairman of the Liberal Party and of the Economic Committee of the Council of Europe. Thanks to their
united support, a strong Danish delegation was assured.

After seeing Retinger off in the 'plane from Copenhagen,
I flew to Switzerland to visit Mr Petitpierre, the President
and Minister of Foreign Affairs, whom I had known for
many years. Thanks to his assistance a first-class delegation
of employers and trade-unionists, representing both the
German- and French-speaking groups, promised to attend.

Delegations from other countries were arranged by my
getting one leading personality from each country to be
responsible for organising both an industrial and trade-
union delegation. Louis Camu, president of the Banque de
Bruxelles, organised the Belgian delegation. Dr A. Pirelli,
founder of the famous Pirelli Company, became head of the
Italian delegation. Professor Meinberg, from the Deutsche

Bank, and Ludwig Rosenberg, chairman of the German T.U.C., arranged the German delegation. I asked Mr Robert Schuman, former Prime Minister and chairman of the European Movement, to speak on the opening day, and through him arranged for an influential French delegation to attend.

Having obtained strong support from the Continent, my task at home was made easy. The British delegation to the conference finally included fifty leading industrial and trade-union leaders, and all the British employers' organisations rallied round under the chairmanship of Lord Knollys. Lord McCorquodale, chairman of the British Employers' Confederation, and Sir Norman Kipping of the Federation of British Industries, each made a significant contribution to the conference. Mr Alan Birch was chairman of the Trades-Union group, which included Mr Frank Cousins, Mr W. J. Carron and Miss Anne Godwin, later to become president of the T.U.C.

Being chairman of what I believe to have been the first international conference ever held composed solely of leaders of industry and trade-unions, I was fulfilling a youthful ambition since, as a young man, I had been on the Secretariat of the International Labour Office of the League of Nations, whose activities were directed towards greater co-operation between employers and trade-unions. The occasion was further enhanced by Derick Heathcoat Amory, the Chancellor of the Exchequer's friendly reference in his opening speech, to the days when we were both under-graduates at Christ Church, Oxford.

In addition to the actual activities of the conference, dinners on the first two evenings enabled British ministers and members of the Labour Party to speak to an even wider circle and obtain general publicity for the problems dis-cussed at the conference. Mr Reginald Maudling, who was negotiating the Free Trade Area proposals, spoke at the first dinner given by me, and Sir David Eccles, President of

o

the Board of Trade, spoke at the second dinner given by Lord Knollys.

Though the Free Trade Area was finally rejected by the French, it may have proved a necessary educational mile-stone in Britain's progress towards a greater understanding of the necessity of her closer integration with Europe.

Having failed in her negotiations with Common Market countries, Britain set about forming the European Free Trade Area (E.F.T.A.), an economic union of Britain, Norway, Sweden, Denmark, Austria, Portugal and Switzer-land. Tariff-barriers were to be abolished between these seven countries, but outside customs-duties were to remain the same. This was not a particularly favourable deal for Britain, as she lowered high customs-duties and offered a large market to her partners, whose existing low tariffs afforded little scope for increased British exports; and she also had to make large agricultural concessions to Denmark. But it was a step forward, however reluctant and hesitating, towards the ideal of European unity.

To help the newly-created E.F.T.A., the United Kingdom Council of the European Movement decided to hold a political and economic conference of the 'seven' in London. So once again I set out on my travels to Scandinavia, Austria, Switzerland and Portugal. In each country I discussed the conference with members of the government, leaders of the opposition, trade-unions and employers. The only excep-tion to this routine was in Portugal, where opposition and free trade-unions are not allowed. Joseph Retinger had wanted to join me in these journeys, but to my dismay I discovered what he had concealed from us all: that he was dying of cancer. One of the last things he did was to help me once again in the arrangements for my various visits, giving his last strength to furthering a cause and an ideal which he had done so much to promote.

My further round of Continental visits gave me quite an insight into the state of party-politics in different countries.

In Scandinavia, as in Britain, pleasant personal relations exist between members of opposing political parties. In Denmark we were particularly anxious that Per Federspiel, leader of the Liberal opposition, should be chairman of their delegation, because he was also at that time chairman of the Council of Europe and spoke perfect English. You have to be extremely tactful in such cases, not to appear to take sides in party-politics, so I asked Mr J. O. Krag, the Foreign Minister, if he had any objection. He warmly supported the idea and said Denmark was proud of Mr Federspiel's position on the Council of Europe.

A very different spirit prevailed in Austria, where the government since the war has been a coalition of Socialists and Conservatives. We had particularly wanted a well-balanced delegation from both parties. Dr Kamitz, the former Conservative Minister of Finance, had just retired from the government after being responsible for the economic rehabilitation of Austrian finances, and was now governor of the Austrian National Bank. He had agreed to come to the conference, and Dr Kreisky, the Foreign Minister and a Socialist, had agreed to speak at my dinner on the first evening. Dr Kreisky is a particularly brilliant man, and was reputed to be largely responsible for negotiating the withdrawal of Russian troops from Austria. But it appeared that, though he and Mr Kamitz had served together for many years in a coalition government, there was no love lost between them, or between their political parties.

To smooth over these difficulties, Sir James Bowker, our Ambassador, had most tactfully invited both Mr Kreisky and Mr Kamitz, and leading members of their parties to meet me at the Embassy. Mr Kamitz, who arrived before some of his colleagues, looking round the room, surprisingly exclaimed, 'Why, there are nothing but Socialists here'. However, thanks to Bowker's initiative and tact, together with the neutral ground on which the discussions took place, a representative delegation of both parties agreed to come to the conference.

To enable this political and economic conference of the 'seven' to obtain a much wider publicity than is accorded to unofficial conferences, we arranged to make it an occasion where leading ministers of the seven countries could express their views. This we did by enabling them to make welcoming speeches on the opening day and to speak at a dinner that evening attended by about five hundred guests. These speeches were publicised throughout Europe on the wireless, on television and in the press. On the British side, Mr Harold Macmillan, the Prime Minister, Mr Selwyn Lloyd, the Chancellor of the Exchequer, Mr Reginald Maudling and Mr Edward Heath, all made important speeches, as did Mr Halvard Lange and Mr Kreisky, Ministers of Foreign Affairs of Norway and Austria, and other leading E.F.T.A. ministers.

The numerous delegates had fruitful discussions in four commissions, covering the main problems to be resolved by the E.F.T.A. grouping. We avoided the preparation of documented reports for the commissions, as is usual on such occasions. Such reports are often out-of-date, take a long time to prepare, and thus delay the holding of the conference. We hit on the novel idea of getting a first class chairman for each committee and asking him to make an opening speech outlining the subjects to be discussed in his committee. The four chairmen were Mr Per Federspiel of Denmark, Dr Walter Boveri of Switzerland, one of the most enlightened and powerful industrialists in Europe and chairman of Brown Boveri, Dr Kamitz of Austria, and finally, the late Mr J. A. Birch, of the T.U.C. who was chairman of the commission on Labour and Social problems. The specialised knowledge of these chairmen made the procedure a signal success.

Like our previous conference, we wasted no time in drafting and redrafting long-winded resolutions, though press conferences were fully informed of the different points of view expressed in the committees.

I thoroughly enjoyed being chairman of this conference, which proved to be the only large political demonstration of E.F.T.A. solidarity. All delegates, though paying lip-service to E.F.T.A., seemed unanimous in stressing that it was only intended as a 'bridge' to enable the eventual union between E.F.T.A. and Common Market countries.

I believe the conference was useful in forcing informed British public opinion to recognise that if it was advisable for Britain to be linked economically to some European countries, then the grouping should be a much larger one than just the E.F.T.A. countries. It also brought into the open the fact that our previous plans for a purely economic union were too timid, and would not prove effective unless strengthened as well by political union. This was coming back to the original dynamic proposals for a united Europe as conceived by Winston Churchill at The Hague Conference. Only such a policy would prove a challenge and an opportunity for Britain in the years to come.

WORKING MEN'S COLLEGE LIBRARY

Chapter Fourteen

★

FARMING AND ARCHAEOLOGY

I NEVER actually intended going into farming. I really drifted into it through my love of horses. My neighbour at Abinger Manor farmed the adjoining 250 acres, working from dawn to dusk with the help of one labourer, an eighteen-year-old tractor and a horse of the same age. Occasionally I helped him by paying for the reseeding of some of his land. In return he let me put up fences between his fields, which in winter enabled me to ride over quite a nice steeplechase course.

One day he told me he had decided to leave as he had insufficient capital to carry on. To save my jumps I offered to take over the lease of his farm, if he would stay on and manage it as my bailiff. At the time I never anticipated the enormous amount of work and expense that this sudden decision would entail.

The landlord of the farm was the Evelyn Estate, which had many thousands of acres inherited from the renowned John Evelyn, the diarist, one of the founders of the Royal Society. Owing to the poor condition of agriculture between the two World wars, the Estate received only a small rent from the farm and had undertaken practically no repairs for years, so the buildings were in a shocking condition, gates were mended by bits of wire, and the main road running down the centre of the farm was almost unusable in winter. The Estate used to earn more from its shooting rights than from its farm rentals, so every few hundred yards good land had been turned into copses as a shelter for pheasants; and with only two men working on my neighbour's large acreage, hedges were no longer trimmed and weeds were prolific. On this type of hilly farm cut into small fields, and under such conditions, a tenant could only manage to scrape a bare living, probably less than the average agricultural wage of the present day.

At that time, just after the War, the government was urging farmers to modernise their farms and increase food production. They offered part-time farmers in the super-tax bracket the inducement of writing off the cost of modernisation from their earnings in non-agricultural pursuits. This influenced me to try to transform these derelict acres into a modern farm. I had always felt that if one lives in the country and enjoys its amenities one must try to make a contribution to agriculture. Here was an opportunity.

So I set to work. The existing buildings were modernised, another labourer's cottage, a new cow-house and two Dutch barns were erected. Changes were made to the approach to the farm so as to beautify it. As I have always thought that pleasant working conditions are a help to efficiency, the cows were milked to the accompaniment of cheerful radio music, and modern reproductions of Renoir adorned the sitting-room of the milk-maid's cottage. The road down the centre of the farm was repaired. The copses were dug up and turned into arable land, and the whole farm was gradually converted into an efficient agricultural unit. I had jumps made between every field and enjoyed, on my rounds of inspection, hopping over them without opening any gates.

As I was used to introducing new labour-saving devices in my industrial undertakings, the farm was soon equipped with the most up-to-date machinery. This included an oil-heated grass-drying machine which turned green grass, when richest in protein, into grass cubes, to be fed to the cattle in winter.

I already had a couple of Guernsey cows for household milk, and being rather attached to them, I decided to go in

for a pedigree Guernsey milking herd. I began to spend all
my spare time pouring over books on cattle-breeding, and
got more and more excited about the idea.

I noted that many of the best Guernsey herds, such as the
Chalvington Herd, had been built up through inbreeding
from one very successful bull, using his sons on the progeny
of the original sire, but had doubts about this policy, which
were reinforced when I met Mrs Cary-Bernard, Ted
Guinness's manager, at the sale of his farm. She had succeeded
in creating a famous herd, without inbreeding, by using
animals only very distantly related. As a result of this
meeting, I asked Mrs Cary-Bernard to come and advise me
on my breeding policy and select the foundation animals of
my herd. This proved a very happy partnership. Later
because of the archaeological discoveries on the farm we
called it Stone-Age Farm, and named the herd Stone-Age.

All my weekends were now spent dealing with a multi-
tude of farm problems. Writing up the pedigree book, I got
to know all the strains of the various Guernsey herds in
England. The detailed farm office work was far more
onerous than being chairman of several important public
companies!

The weekly milk cheque was increased by selling farm-
bottled milk. This of course is a much higher grade than
when pasteurised, as none of the milk's goodness is lost in
the pasteurising process. But it also entails the highest
possible standards in the cleanliness of the cow, constant
tests, and greater mechanisation. The milk flows direct from
the cow's udder through pipes into the bottles, which are
automatically sealed and conveyed to a freezing room,
ready for collection. I had a beautifully illustrated coloured
brochure, which I compiled myself, printed and sent round
by our distributors. I was most interested to hear later from
Alfred Robens, whom I did not know at the time, that he
and his friends at Woldingham had always insisted on
having Stone-Age farm-bottled milk.

The big milk distributors, however, have little interest in promoting specialities like farm-bottled milk. They much prefer to take Guernsey milk, mix it when it suits them with milk with a lower butter-fat content, put it through the pasteurising process, and have done with it.

In the United States, Guernsey producers have organised themselves and created their own distribution and do their own advertising, and so get a much higher price for their higher quality product. In England, the Milk Marketing Board, largely acting as a mere collector of milk, cannot adequately protect the farmer, as the distribution is in the hands of the large combines, who make enormous profits. To my mind the best system is in Denmark, where the Co-operatives buy milk direct from the farmer, and sell it on his behalf, so he retains all the profit.

After seven years, the Stone-Age herd, thanks to Mrs Cary-Bernard, became well known in the Guernsey world, for our bull eventually won the first prize at the Royal Agricultural Show, and so did his progeny. But by this time, the price of pedigree Guernsey cattle had fallen below the cost of rearing them, and the farm was being run at a very substantial loss. Milk production on the lines I had originally planned required large capital expenditure in building and plant and a much bigger labour force than arable and beef production. Also it did not prove profitable on such a small farm, especially when combined with forming a pedigree herd and the extra expense involved in showing.

When the farm eventually became a source of worry, I sold the herd and the farm. I have never minded cutting a loss in business, but I was very sorry to have failed in this experiment due to my lack of experience. In the past I have been used to taking on an unsuccessful business and making it profitable by increasing its turnover. I had not sufficiently realised that such possibilities are restricted in agriculture as there is a limit to what one acre can produce, especially when farming on such a small acreage and on poorish ground.

But I do not regret this experience. Nothing is more exciting than to make something grow where nothing grew before. The former derelict farm is now being successfully run by a yeoman farmer, who has greatly benefited by the improvements I was able to make.

My present home is on a small holding of 40 acres, half a mile from my former farm. I still farm on a modest scale with some Herefords crossed by an Aberdeen Angus bull, and produce eggs and chickens for our own consumption. But my horses no longer demand the extravaganza of my former agricultural experiment!

In the summer of 1949, a young man, armed with a theodolite and various other map-making instruments, called to see me at Abinger Manor. He told me he was working for the Ordnance Survey Authorities and asked if he might look at the mound in the garden which was marked 'Tumulus' on the map. A tumulus is an ancient burial place dating from neolothic times to the late bronze age. He said that this hillock, then overgrown with trees, bushes and bracken, might possibly be a 'Motte', or round earthen fort of the Norman period. He explained that a 'Motte and Bailey' was a type of habitation built after the Norman Conquest; the Motte being a fort with wooden palisades and a wooden tower on the top of a mound, surrounded by a moat, and attached to a Bailey, which was a walled enclosure protecting the habitation of the local knight.

I had never imagined for one moment that the mound in the garden where I had spent so many hours talking to Sydney, while we admired the lovely view spread out below us, was so full of secrets. I immediately got in touch with the Surrey Archaeological Society, who very kindly arranged to help me to have the site fully excavated. Fortunately, the Society was able to persuade young Brian Hope-Taylor, who had just finished another excavation, to undertake the work immediately. So we started work that very summer. First the site was cleared of brushwood, and of all but a few trees near the top, which I was reluctant to cut down, as they looked so beautiful. We then dug a series of trial trenches along the bottom of the mound. These disclosed that the Motte had been formed by earth displaced by the digging of a deep moat. The pond alongside, where we kept goldfish, proved to be part of the ancient moat, which was fed by a natural spring. Further investigation of the moat showed that there had once been a bridge over it. On the top of the Motte, about thirty feet above the moat, careful sifting of the soil revealed the actual darkened wooden post-holes of the surrounding palisade, and of a wooden tower in the centre. Since afforestation on the Surrey hills only began in about Elizabethan times, this tower, 550 feet above sea level, would have had a commanding position in the 11th and 12th centuries, being suitably placed to protect the Bailey, which was on the site now occupied by Abinger Manor. Hope-Taylor made drawings and took photographs of our various discoveries and gradually we cleared all the earth from the surface of the mound, removing the accumulated debris of hundreds of years, until we got it back to its original shape.

The excavation proved particularly rewarding from an archaeological point of view. Very little is known about Mottes, because they were only temporary forts. Some, like the one at Arundel Castle, later became the foundation of a stone tower; others were eventually destroyed by time. This particular Motte, because unnoticed for all these years, was one of the few to have been scientifically investigated under an experienced archaeologist like Hope-Taylor, who later published a detailed account of it under the auspices of the Surrey Archaeological Society.

Eventually the post-holes on the top of the Motte were filled with concrete, and the surface whitewashed, so that the benefits of the work would always be available. The surface of the Motte and moat were carefully turfed over again to retain its original aspect. Floodlit at night, the stems of the tall oak trees near the summit rising above it, to me it is a lovely and mysterious sight.

During excavations on the Motte, Hope-Taylor found several stone age flint implements, which had been thrown up with the earth when the moat was originally dug. He also found 'pot-boilers' or calcinated flints from prehistoric hearths in the kitchen garden. Men in the stone age had evidently selected the site as a desirable one to live on, for the same reasons that had induced the Normans to build the Motte and Bailey, and John Evelyn to build Abinger Manor in Elizabethan times: it was on a high point and had a natural spring.

One day after working on the Motte, Hope-Taylor, Irina and I strolled into the adjoining ploughed field to see if we could find any flints. We had not gone twenty yards before Irina picked one up. Hope-Taylor explained that it was a beautifully shaped bronze-age arrowhead. This was a most exciting moment. In the course of the next half-hour we found dozens of stone implements of every description and realised we were on to something really interesting. This field and all those adjoining were on greensand, which never contains any flint, so any piece of flint found there could only have been left by prehistoric man, perhaps brought from the chalk hills many miles away. In greensand pieces of flint of the stone-age period would naturally lie within a foot or two of the surface, and would be thrown up by the plough.

Each time rain fell I would rush out to continue the treasure hunt, for when it is wet, flint glistens and is easy to spot. Soon many of our friends also became infected with this 'disease', which we called 'Flintomania'. It is a very pleasant pastime. You get plenty of exercise, and the thrill of examining implements left by man on that particular place thousands of years before the dawn of history.

We found arrowheads within shooting distance of the pond, near the Motte, perhaps indicating that the spring not only supplied water for stone-age man, but was also a watering point for wild animals.

All this led me to read an enormous amount about stone-age times, and I became quite expert in differentiating between the artifacts made in the mesolithic, neolithic and bronze ages.

This interest in the stone-age period was given a further impetus when in 1950 I went on a short visit to Kenya to start a pineapple-canning factory. During this visit I became friendly with the famous archaeologist Dr Leakey, head of the Coryndon Museum in Nairobi. He is a man whose qualities I came to admire and whose life is devoted, in a completely disinterested way, to the pursuit of knowledge. He took me to see the many excavations he had made on the dried-up bed of Lake Olorgesaillie in the Rift Valley, and showed me, at different levels, prehistoric sites from palaeolithic to neolithic times. On one site he had erected a primitive building to protect the excavations and all the finds lying *in situ*. I was fascinated to discover that the same types of stone implements found in Surrey had also been fabricated in Equatorial Africa, and the same techniques used.

As I got to study stone-age techniques, I realised that one of the greatest inventions in neolithic times was man's discovery of how to make a polished axe, which for the first time enabled him to cut down a tree. This invention and the gradual evolution of different types of arrowheads, in some inexplicable way, gradually spread throughout the world.

By a strange coincidence Dr and Mrs Leakey spent their next leave at Ewhurst, only a few miles from Abinger. He came over to see the work we had done on the Motte and was so surprised at the quantity of artifacts I had collected and classified that he and Mrs Leakey thought it might be worthwhile to search for a mesolithic site in our fields. We began digging at a spot where I had found a particularly large number of mesolithic flints on the surface, and great was our joy when we eventually found a living site only a few yards away.

The Leakeys and their children, Irina and Serge, and most of our household joined in the excavations. All the earth had to be finely sieved so that every one of the several thousand flints discovered could be carefully noted. On the surface we found mostly bronze-age and neolithic flints, but many of the mesolithic ones were much smaller and lower down. Leakey's explanation of the enormous number of small knife-blades we unearthed was that they were used both for skinning and cutting up animals killed in the chase. Experiments he had carried out in Kenya had shown that an animal about the size of a goat can be completely skinned and cut up by a single small-backed blade less than two inches long, in about twenty minutes.

The result of the excavations was the discovery of a well-preserved mesolithic pit-dwelling, in the form of a large pit in the ground, with post-holes around it, which may have supported a tent-like structure of skins. There were numerous blackened hearths around the pit, and one inside it surrounded by stones.

Dr Leakey and other archaeological experts expressed the view that this was the oldest humanly made and preserved dwelling in the United Kingdom and dated about 8,000 B.C. This period was before England was separated from the Continent by the Channel. Dr Leakey also thought that the field probably contains a number of similar pits.

With the co-operation of Imperial Chemical Industries and Professor Zeuner of the London Institute of Archaeology, chemical experiments were made to preserve the site by hardening it to the consistency of stone, by impregnating the greensand with mixed solutions of water-glass, sodium carbonate and calcium chloride. A light building has been erected above it, where students of archaeology can see the site and examine the finds in the pit, and the other artifacts found in the neighbourhood. Brian Hope-Taylor, who is an artist, as well as an archaeologist, has illustrated the development of the stone-age period in Britain on the walls of the building for the less initiated.

Most weekends in the summer, a continual stream of students visit the museum and look over the Motte.

Chapter Fifteen

★

LIFE BEGINS AT SIXTY

To so many having passed the sixtieth year, life is restricted to an ever-narrowing path. But to a few at that age life unfolds itself on a broader and ever-widening horizon. Experience has taught you to be more appreciative and more tolerant of others; and increased knowledge has enabled you to use your talents to greater advantage. This is how I feel myself, but immeasurably enriched and inspired by a late and romantic marriage.

I have already mentioned how, twenty years previously, I had very much wanted to marry my cousin, Renée, and how our families had opposed our marriage and we had parted. Now, by an extraordinary chain of circumstances, we came together once more. A year after my divorcing Irina a chance meeting brought us into contact. Renée, who had divorced her husband, was at that time living alone with her two children. We both fell in love 'all over again', and this time nothing stood in our way.

Sydney had often told me he knew of no novelist who had written about happy married life. And though his marriage to Violet had been a most perfect one, he never attempted to describe this kind of happiness in a novel. And now I myself realise the difficulty, and why Winston Churchill in his autobiography dismisses the subject with the words, 'and we lived happily ever after'.

I am now experiencing the enchantment of a truly happy marriage, with every interest shared in common. Most of my life I have pursued all my various activities alone and also,

The Motte-Top (looking east) after Phase II
of the excavation of the ground-plan

General view of the Abinger Motte from the south

The author and Renée at Zermatt, 1963

and this is most important, there has been no one except my uncle and aunt with whom I could talk with complete and unreserved freedom. Now talk, real intimate talk, has a great place in personal life, and this continuous conversation on any and every subject, whether serious or trivial, between two people who are *in harmony*, this communion between them is like some subtle warp and weft, two strands which, woven together, form the cloth of happiness.

So Renée and I do not live separate lives in the same house. When I have to talk in public, I read my modest speech to her, we discuss it, make changes, and when the occasion comes to deliver it, I know she is there listening sympathetically. She is informed about all my business activities. When I have to go abroad or visit distant factories, she always accompanies me. As she is a trained singer and also plays the piano, we do a great deal of music together and particularly enjoy singing duets. We go for long rides at our home at Abinger. And then, of course, there is my favourite sport of ski-ing. Since I taught her to ski when she was a girl, I still look upon her as my pupil and that gives me a comfortable feeling of propriety. But above all, we are united in the loving memory of Violet and Sydney who have been such a marvellous and unique inspiration in both our lives.

I am also experiencing something similar to what I had observed in the happy lives of Violet and Sydney. Loving each other so completely, their love overflowed to those near and dear to them. And thus I find my capacity for friendship and devotion has increased in intensity and understanding.

The complete harmony of my personal life has coincided with the fulfilment of another of my aspirations. It was a great day for me when in July last the Prime Minister announced Britain's application to enter the Common Market. It brought nearer the realisation of my most cherished dream, for I have devoted many years and much strenuous endeavour to furthering the cause of a united Europe.

I remember my sixty-fifth birthday as one of the happiest days of my life. We were at Saanenmöser in Switzerland with my dear old friend and guide, William Perren. Since a ski-ing accident some years ago, an osteo-arthritis of one hip has made sport more difficult for me. However, I have taught myself to ride side-saddle, so that I can still hunt, and I enjoy ski-ing as in the past, even if I now have to go steadily and use short, steel skis, instead of the fast, racing-skis of former years.

Well, on my birthday this year the snow conditions were perfect. There was a bright blue sky and the sun shone on the glistening snow. Renée and I, behind William, were turning gently down the slopes, the tall pine trees, their branches heavy with snow, casting deep, purple shadows across the whiteness. Suddenly there was a rushing sound of skiers behind us and there was my son Serge, now taller than myself, beside my stepson Stephen, an undergraduate at Christ Church, my old college, and Serge's most intimate friend, flanked on the other side by my stepdaughter Evelyn, all three practising the 'Wedel' and laughing merrily as they swished to a sudden and skilful stop beside us.

The light-heartedness of the children, the delight of our all ski-ing together, combined with the presence of my dear guide William, made me feel with a sudden stab of intensity that life had no greater joys to offer.

Index

★

WORKING MEN'S COLLEGE LIBRARY

PRINTED IN GREAT BRITAIN
BY ROBERT MACLEHOSE AND CO. LTD
THE UNIVERSITY PRESS, GLASGOW